I0703481

How to Repair Plaster Walls and Create Smooth Surfaces with Skim Coating Techniques

The Ultimate DIY Guide to Fixing Cracks, Holes, and Imperfections in Plaster Walls Using Professional Skim Coating Methods for a Flawless Finish

The Fix It Guy

Table of Contents

Introduction

IHey there, DIY enthusiast! Are you tired of staring at those unsightly cracks, holes, and imperfections in your plaster walls? Do you dream of having smooth, flawless surfaces that look like they were professionally done? Well, you've come to the right place!

As someone who has been through the frustration and heartache of living with damaged plaster walls, I know exactly how you feel. It's like a constant reminder of the work that needs to be done, nagging at you every time you walk into the room. But here's the good news: you don't have to live with those imperfections forever, and you don't have to spend a fortune hiring a professional to fix them!

In this ultimate guide, I'll walk you through the process of repairing your plaster walls yourself using professional skim coating techniques. Not only will you save money by tackling this project on your own, but you'll also experience the incredible satisfaction of transforming your walls with your own two hands. Imagine the pride you'll feel when friends and family marvel at your handiwork!

Now, I know what you might be thinking: "But I've never worked with plaster before! Isn't it complicated and messy?" Trust me, I felt the same way when I first started. But with the right tools, materials, and guidance, anyone can learn to repair plaster walls like a pro. And that's exactly what this book is all about.

We'll start by covering the basics of plaster walls and assessing the damage, so you can determine the scope of work and gather the necessary supplies. Then, we'll dive into step-by-step tutorials for repairing cracks and holes of all sizes, as well as preparing your walls for skim coating. You'll learn the secrets to achieving a flawless finish, with tips and tricks for avoiding common mistakes and troubleshooting any issues that arise.

By the end of this book, you'll have all the knowledge and confidence you need to tackle any plaster wall repair project that comes your way. You'll be able to transform your dingy, damaged walls into smooth, beautiful surfaces that you'll be proud to show off. And best of all, you'll have the satisfaction of knowing that you did it yourself!

So what are you waiting for? Let's get started on your journey to mastering the art of plaster wall repair and skim coating. Trust me, your walls (and your wallet) will thank you!

Chapter 1
Tools and Materials

Essential Tools for Plaster Wall Repair and Skim Coating

Before diving into the nitty-gritty of repairing your plaster walls, it's crucial to ensure you have the right tools on hand. Having the proper equipment will make your job easier, faster, and more efficient, and will help you achieve professional-looking results. In this section, we'll go over the essential tools you'll need for plaster wall repair and skim coating.

1. Putty Knife or Joint Knife

A putty knife or joint knife is a flat, flexible blade with a handle, used for applying and smoothing plaster or joint compound. For plaster wall repair and skim coating, you'll want to have a range of sizes on hand, from a small 1-inch knife for filling tiny cracks to a larger 6-inch knife for covering broader areas. Look for high-quality stainless steel blades with comfortable, ergonomic handles.

2. Taping Knife

A taping knife is similar to a putty knife but typically has a wider, more flexible blade. It's ideal for applying joint tape and skim coating larger surfaces. An 8-inch or 10-inch taping knife is a versatile size for most plaster wall repair projects.

3. Hawk

A hawk is a flat, rectangular tool with a handle, used for holding plaster or joint compound. It allows you to keep your material close at hand while you work, and provides a surface for mixing small batches of compound. Aluminum hawks are lightweight and easy to clean, making them a popular choice among professionals.

4. Trowel

A trowel is a flat, triangular-shaped tool used for applying and smoothing plaster or joint compound. It's ideal for covering larger areas and achieving a smooth, even finish. A 12-inch or 14-inch trowel is a good size for most skim coating projects.

5. Sandpaper and Sanding Blocks

Sandpaper is used for smoothing and feathering the edges of dried plaster or joint compound. You'll want to have a range of grits on hand, from coarse (60-80 grit) for rough shaping to fine (120-150 grit) for final smoothing. Sanding blocks provide a flat, even surface for your sandpaper, making it easier to achieve a smooth finish.

6. Dust Mask and Safety Glasses

Sanding plaster and joint compound creates a lot of fine dust, which can be harmful to breathe in. Always wear a dust mask rated for fine particles (N95 or higher) to protect your lungs. Safety glasses will shield your eyes from dust and debris while you work.

7. Drop Cloths and Plastic Sheeting

Plaster wall repair and skim coating can be messy, so it's essential to protect your floors, furniture, and fixtures from drips and splatters. Use heavy-duty drop cloths or plastic sheeting to cover the area around your workspace, and secure them with painters tape to prevent shifting.

8. Mixing Bucket and Drill with Mixing Paddle

For larger projects, you'll need to mix up batches of plaster or joint compound. A 5-gallon bucket is a good size for most mixing needs. Use a drill with a mixing paddle attachment to blend the material thoroughly, ensuring a smooth, lump-free consistency.

9. Utility Knife and Scissors

A sharp utility knife is handy for cutting joint tape, trimming excess material, and scoring dried compound for removal. Scissors are useful for cutting plastic sheeting and drop cloths to size.

10. Clean-up Tools

Keep a spray bottle filled with water, a damp sponge, and plenty of clean rags on hand for wiping up drips and splatters as you work. A scrub brush and a bucket of warm, soapy water will make cleaning your tools easier at the end of the day.

By gathering these essential tools before starting your plaster wall repair and skim coating project, you'll be well-prepared to tackle any challenges that come your way. In the next section, we'll discuss how to choose the right plaster and skim coating compounds for your specific needs.

Choosing the Right Plaster and Skim Coating Compounds

Now that you have your essential tools ready, it's time to select the appropriate plaster and skim coating compounds for your project. With so many options available on the market, it can be overwhelming to know which products will work best for your specific needs. In this section, we'll break down the different types of plaster and skim coating compounds, and provide guidance on how to choose the right ones for your plaster wall repair project.

Types of Plaster:

1. Gypsum Plaster

Gypsum plaster is the most common type of plaster used in modern construction. It's made from gypsum, a soft mineral that's ground into a fine powder and mixed with water to create a paste. Gypsum plaster is easy to work with, dries quickly, and provides a smooth, durable finish. It's ideal for repairing cracks, holes, and other damage to existing plaster walls.

2. Lime Plaster

Lime plaster is a traditional material that's been used for centuries in construction and decoration. It's made from limestone that's burned and mixed with water and sand to create a paste. Lime plaster is slower to dry than gypsum plaster, but it provides a more breathable, flexible finish that's resistant to cracking and moisture damage. It's often used in historic restoration projects or in areas with high humidity.

3. Cement Plaster

Cement plaster, also known as stucco, is a durable, water-resistant material that's commonly used for exterior walls and other high-moisture areas. It's made from Portland cement, sand, and water, and can be mixed with additives like lime or acrylic fortifiers to improve its strength and flexibility. Cement plaster is not typically used for interior plaster wall repair, but it may be necessary for certain specialized applications.

Types of Skim Coating Compounds:

1. All-Purpose Joint Compound

All-purpose joint compound, also known as drywall mud, is a versatile material that can be used for a variety of repair and finishing tasks. It's made from gypsum, water, and various additives that improve its workability and adhesion. All-purpose joint compound is easy to sand and provides a smooth, seamless finish, making it a popular choice for skim coating plaster walls.

2. Lightweight Joint Compound

Lightweight joint compound is similar to all-purpose compound, but it's formulated with special lightweight additives that make it easier to apply and sand. It's ideal for filling deep cracks or holes, as it minimizes shrinkage and cracking. Lightweight joint compound is also less prone to sagging or slumping, making it a good choice for overhead or vertical applications.

3. Setting-Type Joint Compound

Setting-type joint compound, also known as hot mud, is a fast-drying material that's mixed with water to activate a chemical hardening process. It comes in various setting times, ranging from 5 to 90 minutes, allowing you to choose the appropriate speed for your project. Setting-type joint compound is harder and more durable than regular joint compound, making it ideal for filling deep cracks or holes that require multiple coats. However, it can be more difficult to sand and may require special tools or techniques.

Factors to Consider When Choosing Plaster and Skim Coating Compounds:

1. Compatibility with Existing Materials

When selecting plaster and skim coating compounds, it's essential to choose products that are compatible with the existing materials on your walls. If you're unsure about the type of plaster or substrate you're working with, consult with a professional or perform a small test patch to ensure proper adhesion and compatibility.

2. Drying Time and Workability

Consider the drying time and workability of the products you choose, especially if you're working on a larger project or have limited time available. Faster-setting compounds may be more convenient, but they can also be more challenging to work with and may require more skill to achieve a smooth finish.

3. Sanding and Finishing Properties

Different plaster and skim coating compounds have varying sanding and finishing properties. Some products may be easier to sand and feather out, while others may require more effort or specialized tools. Consider your skill level and the desired final appearance when selecting products.

4. Environmental Factors

Take into account the environmental factors in the room or area where you'll be working, such as humidity, temperature, and ventilation. Some products may perform better in certain conditions than others, so choose accordingly.

5. Cost and Availability

Finally, consider the cost and availability of the plaster and skim coating compounds you're interested in. While it's important to choose high-quality products that will provide lasting results, you also want to stay within your budget and ensure that the materials you need are readily available in your area.

By understanding the different types of plaster and skim coating compounds available, and considering factors like compatibility, workability, finishing properties, environmental conditions, and cost, you'll be well-equipped to choose the right products for your plaster wall repair project. In the next section, we'll discuss how to prepare your work area for optimal safety and efficiency.

Preparing Your Work Area

Before you begin any plaster wall repair or skim coating project, it's crucial to take the time to properly prepare your work area. A well-organized, clean, and safe workspace will make your job easier, more efficient, and more enjoyable. In this section, we'll go over the steps you should take to prepare your work area for optimal results.

1. Clear the Room

Start by removing as much furniture, decor, and other items from the room as possible. This will give you plenty of space to move around and work without obstacles, and will also protect your belongings from dust, debris, and accidental damage. If there are items that are too large or heavy to remove, such as built-in cabinets or appliances, cover them with plastic sheeting and secure the edges with painter's tape.

2. Protect the Floor

Plaster wall repair and skim coating can be messy, with dust, debris, and drips of compound falling onto the floor. To protect your flooring, lay down heavy-duty drop cloths or plastic sheeting across the entire work area. Make sure to overlap the edges of the drop cloths by at least 6 inches, and secure them to the baseboards with painter's tape to prevent shifting or gaps.

3. Cover Electrical Outlets and Switches

Before you begin any sanding or skim coating, make sure to cover all electrical outlets, switches, and fixtures in the room. .

Use painter's tape to secure plastic covers or bags over the openings, ensuring a tight seal to prevent dust and debris from getting inside.

4. Set Up Ventilation

Sanding and mixing plaster and joint compound can create a lot of fine dust particles that can be harmful to breathe in. To minimize dust and improve air quality, set up a portable fan or two in the windows of the room, facing outward. This will help to draw dust and fumes outside, and create a cross-breeze for better ventilation. If possible, open additional windows or doors to further improve air circulation.

5. Gather Your Tools and Materials

Before you begin working, take the time to gather all of the tools and materials you'll need for your project. This may include putty knives, taping knives, hawks, trowels, sandpaper, joint compound, plaster, mixing buckets, and clean-up supplies. Having everything on hand and organized will save you time and frustration later on.

6. Create a Mixing Station

If your project requires mixing plaster or joint compound, set up a dedicated mixing station in a well-ventilated area, preferably outside or in a garage. Use a sturdy table or workbench, and cover the surface with plastic sheeting or a disposable drop cloth. Keep your mixing buckets, water, and tools close at hand, and make sure to wear a dust mask and safety glasses when mixing to protect yourself from inhaling fine particles.

7. Establish a Cleaning Station

Plaster wall repair and skim coating can be messy, so it's important to have a designated area for cleaning your tools and equipment. Set up a large bucket or tub filled with warm, soapy water, and keep plenty of clean rags and sponges on hand. As you work, take breaks to clean your tools and prevent the buildup of dried compound, which can be difficult to remove later.

8. Plan Your Work Sequence

Before you begin, take a few minutes to plan out your work sequence. Identify the areas that need the most attention, and prioritize them based on the severity of the damage and the amount of time and materials required. If possible, work from the top of the room down, and from one end to the other, to minimize the risk of accidentally damaging freshly repaired areas.

9. Don Personal Protective Equipment

Finally, make sure to don appropriate personal protective equipment before beginning any work. This should include a dust mask rated for fine particles (N95 or higher), safety glasses, gloves, and sturdy, closed-toe shoes. If you'll be working on a ladder or scaffold, make sure to follow all safety guidelines and have a spotter on hand to assist you.

By taking the time to properly prepare your work area, you'll create a safer, more efficient, and more enjoyable environment for your plaster wall repair and skim coating project. With your workspace set up and your tools and materials gathered, you'll be ready to tackle any challenges that come your way and achieve professional-looking results

Chapter 2
Repairing Cracks and Holes

Identifying Different Types of Cracks and Holes

Before you begin any plaster wall repair project, it's essential to identify the type and severity of the damage you're dealing with. Different types of cracks and holes require different repair techniques and materials, so understanding what you're up against will help you choose the most effective approach. In this section, we'll go over the most common types of cracks and holes found in plaster walls, and discuss how to identify them.

1. Hairline Cracks

Hairline cracks are the most common type of damage found in plaster walls. These are thin, shallow cracks that often appear in a spiderweb pattern, and are usually caused by normal settling, temperature changes, or minor structural movements. Hairline cracks are generally less than 1/16 inch wide and do not pose a structural threat, but they can be unsightly and may worsen over time if left unrepaired.

To identify hairline cracks, look for thin, jagged lines that are visible on the surface of the plaster. They may be more noticeable in certain lighting conditions, such as when the sun is shining directly on the wall. Hairline cracks will not typically have any accompanying damage, such as flaking or crumbling plaster.

2. Structural Cracks

Structural cracks are more serious than hairline cracks, and are often caused by significant settling, foundation issues, or other structural problems. These cracks are typically wider than 1/16 inch, and may be accompanied by other signs of damage, such as bulging or sagging plaster, or doors and windows that no longer fit properly.

To identify structural cracks, look for deep, wide cracks that run vertically or horizontally across the wall. These cracks may be accompanied by a visible gap or separation between the two sides of the crack, and may widen or narrow as the underlying structural issue shifts. If you suspect that you have structural cracks in your plaster walls, it's important to have them assessed by a professional before attempting any repairs.

3. Impact Damage

Impact damage is caused by a sudden, forceful impact to the plaster wall, such as from a door handle, furniture, or other objects. This type of damage typically results in a localized area of cracking, flaking, or crumbling plaster, and may be accompanied by a visible dent or depression in the wall.

To identify impact damage, look for a concentrated area of damage that is different from the surrounding plaster. The edges of the damaged area may be jagged or uneven, and there may be loose or missing plaster particles. Impact damage can often be repaired using simple patching techniques, but more severe cases may require more extensive repairs.

4. Water Damage

Water damage is a serious issue that can cause significant harm to plaster walls over time. This type of damage is often caused by leaks, floods, or other sources of moisture, and can lead to softening, crumbling, or discoloration of the plaster.

To identify water damage, look for areas of discoloration, staining, or visible moisture on the surface of the plaster. The affected area may feel soft or spongy to the touch, and there may be a musty or damp odor present. In severe cases, the plaster may be visibly crumbling or falling away from the wall. If you suspect that you have water damage in your plaster walls, it's crucial to address the underlying moisture issue before attempting any repairs.

5. Nail or Screw Holes

Nail or screw holes are small, localized holes in the plaster that are caused by the removal of hanging objects, such as pictures, mirrors, or shelves. These holes are typically less than 1/4 inch in diameter and do not pose a structural threat, but they can be unsightly and may detract from the overall appearance of the wall.

To identify nail or screw holes, look for small, circular holes in the plaster that are uniform in size and shape. The edges of the holes may be slightly raised or rough, and there may be a small amount of loose plaster particles around the opening. Nail and screw holes can often be repaired using simple filling techniques, but larger or more numerous holes may require more extensive patching.

By learning to identify the different types of cracks and holes commonly found in plaster walls, you'll be better equipped to choose the most appropriate repair techniques and materials for your project. In the next section, we'll discuss step-by-step methods for repairing small cracks and holes, so you can start restoring your walls to their former glory.

Step-by-Step Guide to Repairing Small Cracks and Holes

Now that you've learned to identify the different types of cracks and holes commonly found in plaster walls, it's time to dive into the repair process. In this section, we'll provide a detailed, step-by-step guide to repairing small cracks and holes, so you can tackle these common issues with confidence.

Materials Needed:
- Joint compound or spackling paste
- Fine-grit sandpaper (120-150 grit)
- Putty knife or taping knife
- Clean, damp cloth or sponge
- Painter's tape (optional)
- Primer and paint (optional)

Step 1: Preparation
Before you begin any repair work, it's essential to properly prepare the area. Start by gently cleaning the crack or hole and the surrounding area with a clean, damp cloth or sponge to remove any dust, dirt, or debris. If there are any loose or flaking bits of plaster, use your putty knife to carefully scrape them away, creating a clean, stable edge around the damage.

Step 2: Filling the Crack or Hole
Once the area is clean and prepped, it's time to fill the crack or hole with joint compound or spackling paste. If you're working with a hairline crack, use your putty knife to apply a thin layer of compound directly into the crack, smoothing it

out as you go. If you're filling a small hole, use your putty knife to apply the compound in a crisscross pattern, building up the material until it's level with the surrounding wall.

Tip: If the crack or hole is deeper than 1/4 inch, you may need to apply the compound in multiple layers, allowing each layer to dry completely before adding the next.

Step 3: Feathering the Edges

After filling the crack or hole, use your putty knife to gently "feather" the edges of the repair, blending the compound seamlessly into the surrounding wall. This will help to create a smooth, even surface and minimize the appearance of the repair.

Tip: If you're having trouble achieving a smooth finish, try dampening your putty knife slightly with water to help the compound spread more easily.

Step 4: Allowing the Compound to Dry

Once you've filled and feathered the crack or hole, allow the joint compound or spackling paste to dry completely. This typically takes between 1-2 hours, depending on the depth of the repair and the humidity in your work area.

Tip: To speed up the drying process, you can use a fan or dehumidifier to circulate air and remove excess moisture.

Step 5: Sanding the Repair

After the compound has dried completely, use a fine-grit sandpaper (120-150 grit) to gently sand the repaired area, smoothing out any rough spots or excess material. Be careful not to sand too aggressively, as this can damage the surrounding plaster.

Tip: To minimize dust and debris, try using a damp sanding sponge instead of traditional sandpaper.

Step 6: Cleaning the Area

Once you've finished sanding, use a clean, damp cloth or sponge to wipe away any dust or debris from the repaired area and the surrounding wall. This will help to create a clean, smooth surface for painting or finishing.

Step 7: Priming and Painting (Optional)

If you plan to paint the repaired area, it's a good idea to prime it first to ensure even coverage and adhesion. Use a high-quality, water-based primer and apply it with a brush or roller, following the manufacturer's instructions. Once the primer has dried completely, you can paint the area to match the surrounding wall.

Tip: If you're not planning to paint the entire wall, use painter's tape to mask off the repaired area before priming and painting to avoid accidentally getting paint on the surrounding plaster.

By following these simple steps, you can effectively repair small cracks and holes in your plaster walls, restoring them to a smooth, seamless finish. With a little patience and practice, you'll be able to tackle these common issues with ease, saving yourself time and money in the process.

Techniques for Fixing Larger Cracks and Holes

While small cracks and holes in plaster walls can often be repaired with simple filling and sanding techniques, larger damage requires a more involved approach. In this section, we'll discuss several techniques for fixing larger cracks and holes, so you can tackle even the most challenging repair projects with confidence.

Technique 1: Patching with Mesh Tape

For cracks or holes that are wider than 1/4 inch, patching with mesh tape can provide added strength and stability to the repair. Here's how to do it:

1. Clean and prepare the area as described in the previous section, removing any loose or flaking plaster.
2. Cut a piece of self-adhesive mesh tape to size, making sure it's long enough to cover the entire crack or hole, plus a few inches on either side.
3. Apply the mesh tape directly over the damage, pressing it firmly into place to ensure good adhesion.
4. Use a putty knife or taping knife to apply a thin layer of joint compound over the mesh tape, smoothing it out as you go.
5. Allow the compound to dry completely, then sand and clean the area as described in the previous section.
6. Apply a second coat of joint compound, feathering the edges to blend the repair seamlessly with the surrounding wall.
7. Allow the second coat to dry, then sand, clean, and prime/paint as desired.

Technique 2: Patching with Backing Material

For holes that are deeper than 1/2 inch, or that have damaged or missing lath (the wooden strips behind the plaster), patching with backing material can help to provide a stable base for the repair. Here's how to do it:

1. Clean and prepare the area as described in the previous section, removing any loose or flaking plaster.
2. Cut a piece of backing material (such as plywood, drywall, or metal lath) to size, making sure it's slightly larger than the hole.
3. Use screws or adhesive to secure the backing material to the lath or studs behind the plaster, creating a stable base for the repair.
4. Apply a layer of joint compound over the backing material, smoothing it out as you go.
5. Allow the compound to dry completely, then sand and clean the area as described in the previous section.
6. Apply a second coat of joint compound, feathering the edges to blend the repair seamlessly with the surrounding wall.
7. Allow the second coat to dry, then sand, clean, and prime/paint as desired.

Technique 3: Patching with Plaster of Paris

For larger cracks or holes that require a stronger, more durable repair, patching with plaster of Paris can be an effective solution. Here's how to do it:

1. Clean and prepare the area as described in the previous section, removing any loose or flaking plaster.

2. Mix a small batch of plaster of Paris according to the manufacturer's instructions, adding water until it reaches a thick, paste-like consistency.

3. Use a putty knife or trowel to apply the plaster of Paris directly into the crack or hole, filling it completely.

4. Use a wet sponge or cloth to smooth out the surface of the plaster, creating a level, even finish.

5. Allow the plaster to dry completely, then sand and clean the area as described in the previous section.

6. If necessary, apply a thin coat of joint compound over the repair to create a seamless finish.

7. Allow the joint compound to dry, then sand, clean, and prime/paint as desired.

Tip: When working with plaster of Paris, it's important to work quickly and efficiently, as the material can begin to harden within minutes of mixing.

By mastering these techniques for fixing larger cracks and holes, you'll be able to tackle even the most challenging plaster wall repairs with ease. Whether you're patching with mesh tape, backing material, or plaster of Paris, the key is to take your time, work carefully, and always prioritize safety and proper preparation. With a little practice and patience, you'll be able to restore your plaster walls to their former glory, creating a smooth, seamless finish that you can be proud of.

Reinforcing Repairs for Long-Lasting Results

While the techniques described in the previous sections are effective for repairing cracks and holes in plaster walls, it's important to take additional steps to reinforce these repairs for long-lasting results. In this section, we'll discuss several methods for reinforcing your plaster repairs, ensuring that they remain strong, stable, and seamless for years to come.

Method 1: Using Fiberglass Mesh Tape
Fiberglass mesh tape is a strong, flexible material that can be used to reinforce plaster repairs, particularly in areas that are prone to movement or stress. Here's how to use it:

1. After filling the crack or hole with joint compound or plaster, allow it to dry completely.
2. Cut a piece of fiberglass mesh tape to size, making sure it's long enough to cover the entire repair, plus a few inches on either side.
3. Apply a thin coat of joint compound over the repair, then immediately press the fiberglass mesh tape into the wet compound.
4. Use a putty knife or taping knife to smooth out the tape, ensuring that it lies flat and adheres well to the surface.
5. Allow the joint compound to dry completely, then apply a second coat over the tape, feathering the edges to blend the repair with the surrounding wall.
6. Allow the second coat to dry, then sand, clean, and prime/paint as desired.

Method 2: Using Plaster Washers

Plaster washers are small, perforated metal discs that can be used to reinforce plaster repairs, particularly in areas where the lath or backing material has been damaged or weakened. Here's how to use them:

1. After filling the crack or hole with joint compound or plaster, allow it to dry completely.
2. Drill small pilot holes around the perimeter of the repair, spacing them evenly and making sure they penetrate into the lath or backing material behind the plaster.
3. Insert plaster washers into each pilot hole, then secure them in place with screws.
4. Apply a thin coat of joint compound over the washers, smoothing it out to create a level surface.
5. Allow the joint compound to dry completely, then apply a second coat, feathering the edges to blend the repair with the surrounding wall.
6. Allow the second coat to dry, then sand, clean, and prime/paint as desired.

Method 3: Using Plaster Bonding Agent

Plaster bonding agent is a liquid adhesive that can be used to improve the bond between fresh plaster and existing plaster, reducing the risk of cracks or separation over time. Here's how to use it:

1. Before filling the crack or hole with plaster, apply a thin coat of plaster bonding agent to the surface of the existing plaster, using a brush or roller.

2. Allow the bonding agent to dry slightly until it becomes tacky, then apply the fresh plaster directly over it.

3. Use a putty knife or trowel to smooth out the plaster, creating a level, even surface.

4. Allow the plaster to dry completely, then sand, clean, and prime/paint as desired.

Tip: When using plaster bonding agent, it's important to follow the manufacturer's instructions carefully, as the drying time and application method may vary depending on the specific product.

Method 4: Using Plaster Buttons

Plaster buttons are small, circular discs made of metal or plastic that can be used to reinforce plaster repairs, particularly in areas where the plaster has separated from the lath or backing material. Here's how to use them:

1. Drill small pilot holes through the plaster and into the lath or backing material, spacing them evenly around the perimeter of the damaged area.

2. Insert plaster buttons into each pilot hole, then secure them in place with screws.

3. Apply a thin coat of joint compound or plaster over the buttons, smoothing it out to create a level surface.

4. Allow the compound or plaster to dry completely, then apply a second coat, feathering the edges to blend the repair with the surrounding wall.

5. Allow the second coat to dry, then sand, clean, and prime/paint as desired.

By using these reinforcement methods in combination with the repair techniques described in the previous sections, you can create strong, durable, and long-lasting repairs that will help to preserve the integrity and beauty of your plaster walls for years to come. Whether you're using fiberglass mesh tape, plaster washers, bonding agent, or plaster buttons, the key is to work carefully and methodically, paying close attention to the specific needs of each repair and the unique characteristics of your plaster walls. With a little practice and patience, you'll be able to master these reinforcement techniques and achieve professional-quality results that you can be proud of.

Chapter 3
Preparing the Surface for Skim Coating

Cleaning and Sanding the Plaster Wall

Before you begin skim coating your plaster walls, it's essential to properly prepare the surface to ensure optimal adhesion and a smooth, seamless finish. In this section, we'll discuss the steps involved in cleaning and sanding your plaster walls, so you can create a solid foundation for your skim coating project.

Step 1: Protecting Your Work Area

Before you begin cleaning and sanding your plaster walls, it's important to protect your work area from dust and debris. Here's what you should do:

1. Remove any furniture, decor, or other items from the room, or cover them with plastic sheeting.
2. Cover the floor with drop cloths or plastic sheeting, securing the edges with painter's tape.
3. Close any doors or windows to prevent dust from spreading to other areas of your home.
4. Put on protective gear, including a dust mask, safety glasses, and gloves.

Step 2: Cleaning the Plaster Wall

Once your work area is protected, you can begin cleaning your plaster walls to remove any dirt, grime, or loose debris. Here's how to do it:

1. Using a soft-bristled brush or broom, gently sweep the entire surface of the wall to remove any loose dust or debris.
2. Mix a solution of warm water and mild detergent in a bucket, then use a sponge or soft cloth to wipe down the wall, starting at the top and working your way down.
3. If there are any particularly stubborn stains or marks, you can use a commercial wall cleaner or a mixture of baking soda and water to gently scrub them away.
4. Once you've cleaned the entire wall, use a clean, damp cloth to wipe away any remaining soap residue.
5. Allow the wall to dry completely before moving on to the next step.

Step 3: Repairing Any Damage

Before you begin sanding your plaster walls, it's important to repair any cracks, holes, or other damage that may be present. Here's what you should do:

1. Using a putty knife or taping knife, fill any cracks or holes with joint compound or plaster, smoothing it out to create a level surface.
2. If there are any particularly large or deep cracks or holes, you may need to use mesh tape or backing material to reinforce the repair, as described in the previous sections.
3. Allow the repair material to dry completely, then sand it smooth using a fine-grit sandpaper (120-150 grit).

Step 4: Sanding the Plaster Wall

Once your plaster walls are clean and repaired, you can begin sanding them to create a smooth, even surface for skim coating. Here's how to do it:

1. Using a medium-grit sandpaper (80-100 grit), gently sand the entire surface of the wall, starting at the top and working your way down.

2. Pay particular attention to any rough or uneven areas, sanding them until they are smooth and level with the surrounding wall.

3. If you encounter any particularly stubborn rough spots or protrusions, you can use a coarser-grit sandpaper (60-80 grit) to remove them, then switch back to a medium-grit sandpaper to smooth out the area.

4. As you sand, be sure to wear a dust mask to avoid inhaling any plaster dust, and use a vacuum or damp cloth to periodically remove any dust from the surface of the wall.

5. Once you've sanded the entire wall, use a fine-grit sandpaper (120-150 grit) to gently sand the surface once more, creating a smooth, even finish.

Step 5: Cleaning Up

After you've finished sanding your plaster walls, it's important to thoroughly clean the area to remove any dust or debris that may interfere with the skim coating process. Here's what you should do:

1. Using a vacuum with a brush attachment, carefully vacuum the entire surface of the wall to remove any loose dust or debris.

2. Wipe down the wall with a clean, damp cloth to remove any remaining dust, then allow it to dry completely.

3. Remove any drop cloths or plastic sheeting from your work area, and carefully dispose of any debris or dust that may have accumulated.

By following these steps to clean and sand your plaster walls, you'll create a smooth, even surface that is well-prepared for skim coating. With your walls properly prepped, you'll be able to achieve a flawless, professional-quality finish that will last for years to come. In the next section, we'll discuss the importance of priming your plaster walls before skim coating, and provide step-by-step instructions for achieving optimal results.

Priming the Surface for Optimal Adhesion

After cleaning and sanding your plaster walls, the next crucial step in preparing for skim coating is priming the surface. Priming helps to seal the plaster, improves adhesion of the skim coat, and creates a uniform surface that will result in a smoother, more even finish. In this section, we'll explore the importance of priming and provide a detailed guide on how to prime your plaster walls for optimal results.

Why Priming is Essential:

1. Sealing the Surface: Plaster is a porous material that can absorb moisture from the skim coat, leading to uneven drying and potential cracking. Priming seals the surface, preventing moisture absorption and ensuring a more consistent drying process.

2. Improving Adhesion: A primer creates a slightly textured surface that provides better grip for the skim coat, ensuring better adhesion and reducing the risk of the skim coat peeling or flaking off over time.

3. Creating a Uniform Surface: Plaster walls may have variations in color and texture, which can be visible through the skim coat if not properly primed. A primer helps to create a uniform surface, minimizing any imperfections and ensuring a more even final appearance.

Step 1: Choosing the Right Primer

When selecting a primer for your plaster walls, it's essential to choose a product that is specifically designed for use on plaster surfaces. Here are some factors to consider:

1. Type of Primer: There are two main types of primers suitable for plaster walls: oil-based and water-based. Oil-based primers provide excellent sealing and adhesion properties but have a strong odor and require longer drying times. Water-based primers are more environmentally friendly, have lower odor, and dry faster, making them a popular choice for many DIY enthusiasts.

2. Quality: Choose a high-quality primer from a reputable manufacturer to ensure optimal performance and longevity. Lower-quality primers may not provide adequate sealing or adhesion, leading to issues with your skim coat down the line.

3. Tintable Primers: If you plan to paint your walls after skim coating, consider using a tintable primer. These primers can be tinted to match your final paint color, reducing the number of coats needed and providing a more seamless finish.

Step 2: Preparing the Primer

Before applying the primer to your plaster walls, it's essential to prepare it according to the manufacturer's instructions. Here's what you should do:

1. Stir the primer thoroughly to ensure that any settled pigments are evenly distributed throughout the mixture.

2. If using a tintable primer, add the appropriate amount of colorant and mix well until the color is consistent throughout.

3. If the primer is too thick, you may need to thin it slightly with water or the appropriate solvent, following the manufacturer's guidelines for the correct ratio.

Step 3: Applying the Primer

Once your primer is prepared, you're ready to apply it to your plaster walls. Here's how to do it:

1. Pour the primer into a paint tray, and using a high-quality roller cover (3/8" to 1/2" nap), apply the primer to the wall in a "W" pattern, starting at the bottom and working your way up.

2. Overlap each pass by about 50% to ensure even coverage, and maintain a wet edge to avoid visible lap marks.

3. Use a high-quality brush to cut in around the edges, corners, and any trim or fixtures.

4. Allow the primer to dry completely according to the manufacturer's recommended drying time, which may vary depending on humidity and temperature.

5. If necessary, apply a second coat of primer, following the same technique as the first coat.

Step 4: Inspecting the Primed Surface

After the primer has dried completely, carefully inspect the surface of your plaster walls for any imperfections or missed spots. Here's what to look for:

1. Uneven Coverage: Check for any areas where the primer may have been applied too thinly or missed altogether. These areas will require additional primer before proceeding with the skim coat.

2. Drips or Runs: Look for any drips, runs, or sagging in the primer, particularly in corners or along edges. These imperfections should be sanded smooth and recoated with primer before skim coating.

3. Texture: Run your hand over the primed surface to check for any rough spots or unevenness. If necessary, lightly sand these areas with a fine-grit sandpaper (120-150 grit) to create a smooth, even surface.

By properly priming your plaster walls, you'll create an ideal surface for your skim coat, ensuring better adhesion, a more even finish, and a longer-lasting result. With your walls cleaned, sanded, and primed, you're now ready to move on to the next stage of your skim coating project: masking and protecting adjacent areas, which we'll cover in detail in the following section.

Masking and Protecting Adjacent Areas

Before beginning the skim coating process, it's crucial to properly mask and protect any adjacent areas that you want to keep free from joint compound or plaster. This includes baseboards, trim, windows, doors, and any other surfaces that may be difficult to clean if accidentally splattered. In this section, we'll discuss the importance of masking and provide a step-by-step guide to protecting your adjacent areas for a clean, professional-looking finish.

Why Masking is Important:

1. Keeping Adjacent Areas Clean: Skim coating can be a messy process, and joint compound or plaster can easily splatter or drip onto nearby surfaces. By masking these areas, you'll keep them clean and free from unwanted residue.

2. Saving Time on Cleanup: Properly masking your adjacent areas will save you significant time and effort in the cleanup process. Instead of scraping or sanding away dried joint compound from your trim or baseboards, you can simply remove the masking tape and protective coverings for a clean, crisp edge.

3. Achieving a Professional Look: Masking creates sharp, defined lines between your skim-coated surface and the adjacent areas, resulting in a polished, professional appearance.

Step 1: Gathering Your Masking Materials

Before you begin masking, make sure you have the following materials on hand:

1. Painter's Tape: Choose a high-quality painter's tape that is designed for use on delicate surfaces and provides a strong, reliable seal. Blue tape or green Frog Tape are popular options.

2. Plastic Sheeting or Masking Film: Thin plastic sheeting or masking film will protect larger surfaces like windows, doors, or built-in fixtures from joint compound splatters.

3. Scissors or Utility Knife: You'll need scissors or a sharp utility knife to cut your masking materials to size.

4. Masking Paper or Brown Builder's Paper: Masking paper or brown builder's paper is ideal for covering and protecting floors or large expanses of wall that won't be skim-coated.

Step 2: Applying Painter's Tape
Begin the masking process by applying painter's tape to the edges of any trim, baseboards, or other surfaces that abut the area to be skim-coated. Here's how to do it:

1. Ensure that the surfaces are clean and dry before applying the tape.

2. Starting at one end, apply the painter's tape along the edge of the trim or baseboard, pressing it down firmly to create a tight seal. Overlap the tape slightly at the corners to ensure full coverage.

3. Use your fingernail or a putty knife to gently press the edge of the tape into any crevices or details in the trim for a more precise seal.

4. Continue applying the tape along the entire length of the trim or baseboard, making sure to maintain a straight, even line.

Step 3: Covering Windows, Doors, and Fixtures
After taping off your trim and baseboards, move on to masking any windows, doors, or built-in fixtures in the room. Here's how to do it:

1. Cut your plastic sheeting or masking film to size, allowing enough excess to cover the entire surface and overlap the edges slightly.

2. Use painter's tape to secure the plastic sheeting or film to the surrounding walls or trim, creating a tight seal around the perimeter of the window, door, or fixture.

3. If necessary, use additional strips of painter's tape to secure the center of the plastic sheeting or film to the surface, preventing it from billowing or sagging.

Step 4: Protecting Floors and Large Wall Areas
Finally, cover and protect your floors and any large wall areas that won't be skim-coated using masking paper or brown builder's paper. Here's how to do it:

1. Roll out the masking paper or builder's paper along the length of the wall or floor, allowing enough excess to cover the entire surface and overlap the edges slightly.

2. Use painter's tape to secure the edges of the paper to the baseboards, trim, or adjacent walls, creating a tight seal around the perimeter.

3. If covering a large expanse of floor, use additional strips of painter's tape to secure the seams between sheets of paper, preventing them from shifting or gapping.

4. When covering walls, use a straightedge or level to ensure that the top edge of the paper is straight and even.

Step 5: Double-Checking Your Masking

Before beginning your skim coating project, take a moment to double-check your masking work. Here's what to look for:

1. Gaps or Loose Edges: Check for any gaps or loose edges in your painter's tape or protective coverings that may allow joint compound or plaster to seep through.

2. Secure Adhesion: Ensure that all of your masking materials are securely adhered to the surfaces and won't come loose during the skim coating process.

3. Full Coverage: Verify that you've completely covered and protected all adjacent areas that you want to keep clean.

By taking the time to properly mask and protect your adjacent areas before skim coating, you'll not only achieve a cleaner, more professional-looking finish but also save yourself significant time and effort in the cleanup process. With your surfaces fully prepped and masked, you're now ready to dive into the heart of your skim coating project, which we'll cover in detail in the upcoming chapters.

Chapter 4
Skim Coating Techniques
Mixing the Skim Coating Compound

Properly mixing your skim coating compound is essential for achieving a smooth, consistent texture and ensuring optimal adhesion to your plaster walls. In this section, we'll discuss the importance of proper mixing and provide a detailed guide on how to mix your skim coating compound for the best results.

Why Proper Mixing is Crucial:

1. Consistency: Thoroughly mixing your skim coating compound ensures a smooth, lump-free consistency that will apply evenly and dry to a seamless finish.

2. Adhesion: Properly mixed skim coating compound will bond more effectively to your primed plaster walls, reducing the risk of cracking, peeling, or flaking over time.

3. Workability: A well-mixed skim coating compound will be easier to apply and work with, allowing you to achieve a more professional-looking finish with less effort.

Step 1: Choosing Your Skim Coating Compound
Before mixing, select the appropriate skim coating compound for your project. There are two main types to choose from:

1. Setting-Type Compound: Also known as "hot mud," setting-type compounds are mixed with water and harden through a chemical reaction.

They offer faster drying times and are ideal for filling deeper imperfections or achieving a thick, durable finish.

2. Drying-Type Compound: Also called "pre-mixed" or "ready-mixed" compounds, these products come in a paste form and harden through evaporation. They offer longer working times and are better suited for thinner coats and smoother finishes.

Consider the specific needs of your project, such as the depth of imperfections, desired drying time, and final texture when selecting your skim coating compound.

Step 2: Gathering Your Mixing Tools
To mix your skim coating compound, you'll need the following tools:

1. Mixing Container: Use a clean, sturdy container large enough to accommodate the amount of compound you need to mix. A 5-gallon bucket is suitable for most projects.

2. Mixing Paddle: A mixing paddle attached to a drill will make mixing your compound much easier and more efficient than stirring by hand. Choose a paddle with a diameter appropriate for your mixing container.

3. Drill: Use a corded or cordless drill with sufficient power to turn the mixing paddle through the thick compound mixture.

4. Clean Water: Have a supply of clean, room-temperature water on hand for mixing. Avoid using hot water, as it can cause the compound to dry too quickly.

Step 3: Mixing the Skim Coating Compound
Now that you have your tools and materials ready, follow these steps to mix your skim coating compound:

1. Pour the desired amount of clean, room-temperature water into your mixing container. Refer to the manufacturer's instructions for the recommended water-to-compound ratio.

2. Gradually add the skim coating compound to the water, sprinkling it evenly across the surface to prevent clumping.

3. Allow the mixture to sit for a few minutes to allow the compound to absorb the water. This process, called "slaking," helps to ensure a smoother, more homogeneous mixture.

4. Insert your mixing paddle into the compound mixture, ensuring that it reaches the bottom of the container.

5. Begin mixing the compound at a low speed, gradually increasing the speed as the mixture becomes more homogeneous. Mix for the amount of time recommended by the manufacturer, typically 2-5 minutes.

6. Scrape the sides and bottom of the container with a margin trowel or putty knife to ensure that all of the compound is fully incorporated.

7. Continue mixing until the compound reaches a smooth, lump-free consistency similar to thick pancake batter. Adjust the consistency as needed by adding small amounts of water or compound until you achieve the desired texture.

Step 4: Testing the Consistency
Before applying your mixed skim coating compound, test its consistency to ensure that it's suitable for your project. Here's how:

1. Scoop a small amount of the mixed compound onto a putty knife or trowel and hold it vertically.

2. Observe how the compound falls off the blade. It should flow smoothly and evenly, creating a thick, continuous ribbon.

3. If the compound is too thick, it will cling to the blade and resist falling off. In this case, add small amounts of water, mixing thoroughly, until the desired consistency is achieved.

4. If the compound is too thin, it will drip or run off the blade quickly. Add small amounts of dry compound, mixing thoroughly, until the desired consistency is reached.

By properly mixing your skim coating compound, you'll ensure a smooth, consistent texture that will adhere well to your plaster walls and dry to a seamless, professional-looking finish. With your compound mixed and ready, you can now move on to the application process, which we'll cover in detail in the following sections.

Applying the First Coat of Skim Coating

After properly mixing your skim coating compound, it's time to begin applying the first coat to your plaster walls. This initial layer will help to fill in any remaining imperfections, even out the surface texture, and create a smooth base for the subsequent coats. In this section, we'll provide a detailed guide on how to apply the first coat of skim coating for optimal results.

Tools and Materials Needed:
1. Mixed Skim Coating Compound
2. Hawk or Mud Pan
3. Taping Knife or Trowel (10-12 inches)
4. Putty Knife or Trowel (4-6 inches)
5. Sanding Block or Sanding Pole with 120-150 Grit Sandpaper
6. Clean, Damp Sponge or Rag

Step 1: Loading Your Hawk or Mud Pan
Begin by loading your hawk or mud pan with a generous amount of the mixed skim coating compound. Here's how:

1. Use a large putty knife or trowel to scoop a substantial amount of the mixed compound onto your hawk or into your mud pan.

2. Spread the compound evenly across the surface of the hawk or mud pan, creating a mound that's easy to access with your taping knife or trowel.

3. Avoid overloading your hawk or mud pan, as this can make it difficult to control the amount of compound you apply to the wall.

Step 2: Applying the First Coat

With your hawk or mud pan loaded, follow these steps to apply the first coat of skim coating:

1. Start at a top corner of the wall and work your way down and across in a systematic pattern.

2. Hold your taping knife or trowel at a 45-degree angle to the wall surface, with the blade slightly flexed to create a smooth, even pressure.

3. Load your taping knife or trowel with compound from your hawk or mud pan, then apply it to the wall using long, smooth strokes. Overlap each pass by about 50% to ensure even coverage.

4. Use a light to moderate pressure when applying the compound, allowing it to fill in any imperfections and create a thin, even layer across the surface.

5. As you work, periodically clean your taping knife or trowel with a damp sponge or rag to prevent the buildup of dried compound.

6. For hard-to-reach areas or tight corners, use a smaller putty knife or trowel to apply the compound, using the same overlapping stroke technique.

Step 3: Smoothing the First Coat

After applying the first coat of skim coating compound, go back over the surface to smooth out any ridges, lines, or inconsistencies. Here's how:

1. Hold your taping knife or trowel at a low angle to the wall surface, with the blade almost flat against the compound.

2. Using light pressure, glide the blade over the surface in long, even strokes, filling in any low spots and removing any excess compound.

3. Work in a systematic pattern, overlapping each pass to ensure a smooth, even finish.

4. Avoid overworking the compound, as this can lead to gouging or pulling the material away from the wall surface.

Step 4: Letting the First Coat Dry

Once you've applied and smoothed the first coat of skim coating compound, allow it to dry completely before proceeding to the next step. Here's what to keep in mind:

1. Drying times will vary depending on the type of compound used, the thickness of the coat, and the ambient humidity and temperature.

2. Refer to the manufacturer's instructions for estimated drying times, but generally, allow at least 4-8 hours for the first coat to dry thoroughly.

3. Avoid applying additional coats or sanding the surface until the first coat is completely dry to the touch.

Step 5: Sanding the First Coat (if needed)
In some cases, you may need to lightly sand the first coat of skim coating compound before applying subsequent coats. Here's when and how to sand:

1. If the dried first coat has any noticeable ridges, lines, or rough patches, use a sanding block or sanding pole with 120-150 grit sandpaper to lightly sand the surface.

2. Sand in a circular motion, applying even pressure across the entire surface to create a smooth, level base for the next coat.

3. Avoid over-sanding, as this can remove too much of the compound and expose the underlying plaster surface.

4. After sanding, use a clean, damp sponge or rag to wipe away any dust or debris from the surface before applying the next coat.

By carefully applying and smoothing the first coat of skim coating compound, you'll create an even, uniform base that will help to ensure a smooth, professional-looking finish. With the first coat complete, you can move on to applying additional coats to refine the surface further, which we'll cover in detail in the next section.

Sanding and Smoothing the First Coat

After applying the first coat of skim coating compound and allowing it to dry completely, the next crucial step is to sand and smooth the surface in preparation for subsequent coats. Proper sanding helps to remove any imperfections, ridges, or unevenness, creating a level base that will ensure a smooth, seamless finish. In this section, we'll provide a detailed guide on how to effectively sand and smooth the first coat of skim coating compound.

Tools and Materials Needed:
1. Sanding Block or Sanding Pole
2. 120-150 Grit Sandpaper
3. Dust Mask
4. Safety Glasses
5. Shop Vacuum or Dust Collector
6. Clean, Damp Sponge or Rag

Step 1: Preparing Your Work Area
Before beginning the sanding process, take a few minutes to prepare your work area. Here's what to do:

1. Cover any furniture, floors, or fixtures in the room with drop cloths or plastic sheeting to protect them from dust.

2. Ensure that your work area is well-ventilated by opening windows and setting up fans to help circulate air and remove dust particles.

3. Put on a dust mask and safety glasses to protect yourself from fine dust particles during sanding.

4. Set up a shop vacuum or dust collector nearby to help minimize the amount of airborne dust.

Step 2: Selecting the Right Sandpaper
Choosing the appropriate grit of sandpaper is essential for achieving the best results when sanding your first coat of skim coating compound. Here's what to consider:

1. For most skim coating applications, 120-150 grit sandpaper is ideal. This grit range is fine enough to remove imperfections and create a smooth surface without removing too much of the compound.

2. If your first coat has significant ridges, bumps, or unevenness, you may need to start with a coarser grit, such as 100-120, before moving on to a finer grit for the final smoothing.

3. Avoid using sandpaper with a grit higher than 150, as this may create an overly smooth surface that doesn't provide enough tooth for subsequent coats to adhere properly.

Step 3: Sanding the First Coat
With your work area prepared and the appropriate sandpaper selected, follow these steps to sand the first coat of skim coating compound:

1. Begin by lightly sanding the entire surface using a sanding block or sanding pole with 120-150 grit sandpaper.

2. Sand in a circular motion, applying even pressure across the surface to remove any ridges, bumps, or imperfections.

3. Periodically check your progress by running your hand over the surface to feel for any rough spots or unevenness.

4. Pay extra attention to edges, corners, and hard-to-reach areas, using a smaller sanding block or folded piece of sandpaper to ensure a uniform finish.

5. As you sand, the compound will create a fine dust. Use your shop vacuum or dust collector to periodically remove this dust from the surface and surrounding areas.

Step 4: Smoothing the Surface
After sanding the first coat, take a few additional steps to further smooth and refine the surface:

1. Use a clean, damp sponge or rag to wipe the entire surface, removing any remaining dust or debris.

2. As you wipe the surface, feel for any rough spots or imperfections that may require additional sanding.

3. If you find any areas that need more attention, use a smaller piece of sandpaper to spot-sand those specific areas until they blend seamlessly with the surrounding surface.

4. Once you're satisfied with the smoothness and uniformity of the surface, give it a final wipe with a clean, damp sponge or rag to remove any remaining dust particles.

Step 5: Inspecting the Surface

Before moving on to applying subsequent coats of skim coating compound, take a moment to carefully inspect the sanded and smoothed surface:

1. Use a bright light held at a low angle to the surface to highlight any imperfections, ridges, or unevenness that may still be present.

2. Run your hand over the surface to feel for any rough spots or inconsistencies in texture.

3. If you find any areas that need further sanding or smoothing, address them now before proceeding to the next coat.

4. Once you're satisfied with the quality and uniformity of the surface, you can move on to applying additional coats of skim coating compound.

By properly sanding and smoothing the first coat of skim coating compound, you'll create an ideal surface for subsequent coats to adhere to, ensuring a smooth, professional-looking finish. The time and effort invested in this crucial step will pay off in the form of a flawless, seamless surface that will last for years to come. In the next section, we'll discuss the process of applying additional coats of skim coating compound to further refine and perfect your plaster walls.

Applying Additional Coats for a Flawless Finish

After sanding and smoothing the first coat of skim coating compound, you're ready to apply additional coats to further refine the surface and achieve a flawless finish. Each subsequent coat helps to fill in any remaining imperfections, create a more uniform texture, and build up a smooth, durable surface that will stand the test of time. In this section, we'll provide a detailed guide on how to apply additional coats of skim coating compound for optimal results.

Tools and Materials Needed:
1. Mixed Skim Coating Compound
2. Hawk or Mud Pan
3. Taping Knife or Trowel (10-12 inches)
4. Putty Knife or Trowel (4-6 inches)
5. 150-220 Grit Sandpaper
6. Sanding Block or Sanding Pole
7. Clean, Damp Sponge or Rag

Step 1: Preparing the Surface
Before applying the second coat of skim coating compound, ensure that the surface is properly prepared. Here's what to do:

1. Remove any dust or debris from the sanded and smoothed first coat using a clean, damp sponge or rag.

2. Allow the surface to dry completely before proceeding.

3. Inspect the surface once more for any imperfections or unevenness that may require additional sanding or smoothing.

4. If necessary, lightly sand any problem areas with 150-grit sandpaper and wipe away any dust before moving on.

Step 2: Mixing and Applying the Second Coat

With the surface prepared, mix a fresh batch of skim coating compound and apply the second coat using the following technique:

1. Load your hawk or mud pan with the mixed compound, as described in the previous section.

2. Using a taping knife or trowel, apply a thin, even layer of compound over the entire surface, using long, smooth strokes.

3. Overlap each pass by about 50% to ensure consistent coverage and a uniform texture.

4. As you apply the second coat, focus on filling in any remaining imperfections or low spots, using a slightly thicker application of compound in those areas.

5. Feather the edges of the second coat to blend seamlessly with the surrounding surface.

6. Once you've covered the entire area, go back over the surface with your taping knife or trowel, using long, even strokes to smooth out any ridges or unevenness.

Step 3: Sanding the Second Coat

After the second coat has dried completely (refer to the manufacturer's instructions for drying times), sand the surface to achieve an even smoother finish:

1. Using a sanding block or sanding pole with 150-grit sandpaper, lightly sand the entire surface in a circular motion.

2. Apply even pressure to remove any minor imperfections, ridges, or brush strokes.

3. Periodically wipe away any dust with a clean, damp sponge or rag to assess your progress and ensure a consistent finish.

4. Once you've achieved a smooth, uniform surface, wipe away any remaining dust with a damp sponge or rag.

Step 4: Applying Additional Coats (if needed)

In some cases, particularly for heavily damaged or uneven plaster walls, you may need to apply a third or even fourth coat of skim coating compound to achieve the desired level of smoothness and uniformity. If additional coats are necessary:

1. Repeat the process of mixing, applying, and sanding the compound, as described in steps 2 and 3.

2. With each subsequent coat, use a slightly thinner application of compound and a finer grit of sandpaper (up to 220-grit) to refine the surface further.

3. Continue applying coats until you're satisfied with the overall smoothness, uniformity, and quality of the surface.

Step 5: Final Sanding and Inspection

After applying the final coat of skim coating compound and allowing it to dry completely, perform a final sanding and inspection:

1. Using a sanding block or sanding pole with 220-grit sandpaper, lightly sand the entire surface in a circular motion to achieve an ultra-smooth finish.

2. Wipe away any dust with a clean, damp sponge or rag, and inspect the surface carefully under bright light.

3. Look for any remaining imperfections, ridges, or unevenness, and spot-sand those areas if necessary.

4. Once you're satisfied with the final result, wipe the surface one last time with a damp sponge or rag to remove any dust.

By applying additional coats of skim coating compound and carefully sanding and smoothing each layer, you'll achieve a flawless, professional-grade finish that will transform your plaster walls. The key to success is patience, attention to detail, and a willingness to put in the time and effort required to create a truly outstanding result. With practice and perseverance, you'll be able to master the art of skim coating and take pride in your beautifully restored plaster walls for years to come.

Tips and Tricks for Achieving Professional Results

Achieving professional-looking results when skim coating plaster walls requires a combination of the right techniques, tools, and a keen eye for detail. In this section, we'll share some valuable tips and tricks that will help you elevate your skim coating skills and create a finish that rivals that of a seasoned pro.

1. Start with a Clean, Dry Surface

Before beginning any skim coating project, ensure that your plaster walls are clean, dry, and free from any dust, debris, or loose material. A clean surface will help the skim coating compound adhere properly and create a more uniform finish.

2. Use High-Quality Tools

Invest in high-quality tools, such as stainless steel taping knives, trowels, and hawks. These tools will provide better control, smoother application, and more consistent results than cheaper, lower-quality alternatives.

3. Mix Compound to the Right Consistency

When mixing your skim coating compound, aim for a consistency that is smooth, creamy, and easy to apply without being too runny or too thick. A properly mixed compound will help minimize air bubbles, reduce the risk of cracking, and create a more even finish.

4. Apply Thin, Even Coats

When applying skim coating compound, focus on creating thin, even coats rather than trying to fill in all imperfections at once. Thin coats dry more quickly, are easier to sand, and will result in a smoother, more professional-looking finish.

5. Use Long, Smooth Strokes

As you apply the skim coating compound, use long, smooth strokes with your taping knife or trowel to create a consistent texture and minimize the appearance of edges or ridges. Overlap each pass by about 50% to ensure even coverage.

6. Feather the Edges

When applying skim coating compound near edges, corners, or transitions, use a light touch and feather the material to create a seamless blend with the surrounding surface. This technique helps to minimize the appearance of hard lines or demarcations.

7. Allow Adequate Drying Time

Be patient and allow each coat of skim coating compound to dry completely before sanding or applying subsequent coats. Rushing the drying process can lead to cracking, flaking, or an uneven finish.

8. Sand Between Coats

Sanding between each coat of skim coating compound is crucial for achieving a smooth, professional-looking finish. Use a sanding block or sanding pole with progressively finer grits of sandpaper (120-grit to 220-grit) to remove imperfections and create a uniform surface texture.

9. Use a Damp Sponge for Final Smoothing

After the final coat of skim coating compound has dried and been sanded, use a clean, damp sponge to gently smooth the surface and remove any remaining dust or debris. This final step helps to create an ultra-smooth finish and prepares the surface for priming and painting.

10. Inspect Your Work Under Different Lighting Conditions

To ensure that your skim coated walls are as smooth and flawless as possible, inspect your work under different lighting conditions, such as natural daylight, overhead lighting, and angled lighting. This will help you spot any imperfections or inconsistencies that may be less visible under certain lighting conditions.

11. Practice Patience and Persistence

Achieving professional-looking results when skim coating plaster walls takes time, practice, and patience. Don't get discouraged if your first attempts aren't perfect; with persistence and a willingness to learn from your mistakes, you'll continually improve your skills and create increasingly impressive results.

12. Maintain a Clean Work Area

Throughout the skim coating process, maintain a clean and organized work area. Clean your tools regularly, dispose of any debris or dust promptly, and keep your work surface free from clutter. A clean work area will help you stay focused, efficient, and produce better results.

By incorporating these tips and tricks into your skim coating practice, you'll be well on your way to achieving professional-grade results that will impress friends, family, and clients alike. Remember, the key to success is a combination of the right tools, techniques, and a commitment to continuous improvement. With time and dedication, you'll be able to transform even the most challenging plaster walls into smooth, flawless surfaces that showcase your skill and craftsmanship.

Chapter 5
Finishing Touches
Priming and Painting the Repaired Plaster Wall

After successfully repairing and skim coating your plaster walls, the final step in achieving a flawless, professional-looking finish is to prime and paint the surface. Priming helps to seal the newly repaired surface, providing a uniform base for the paint to adhere to, while painting protects the wall and allows you to customize the color and sheen to your desired aesthetic. In this section, we'll walk you through the process of priming and painting your repaired plaster wall for optimal results.

Tools and Materials Needed:
1. Interior latex primer
2. High-quality interior paint
3. Paint roller and covers (3/8" to 1/2" nap)
4. Paint tray and liner
5. Angled paintbrush (2" to 2.5")
6. Extension pole (if needed)
7. Drop cloths or plastic sheeting
8. Painter's tape
9. Clean, damp cloth or sponge

Step 1: Preparing the Room
Before beginning the priming and painting process, take the time to properly prepare your work area:

1. Remove any furniture, decor, or fixtures from the room, or cover them with drop cloths or plastic sheeting to protect them from paint drips or splatters.

2. Lay drop cloths or plastic sheeting on the floor, extending a few feet out from the base of the wall to catch any drips or spills.

3. Use painter's tape to mask off any adjacent surfaces, such as baseboards, trim, or windows, to ensure a clean, crisp paint line.

Step 2: Cleaning the Surface

Prior to priming, clean the repaired plaster wall to remove any dust, debris, or contaminants that may interfere with paint adhesion:

1. Using a clean, damp cloth or sponge, gently wipe down the entire surface of the wall, paying extra attention to any areas that were recently sanded or repaired.

2. Allow the surface to dry completely before proceeding with priming.

Step 3: Applying Primer

Applying a quality interior latex primer is essential for creating a uniform surface and ensuring optimal paint adhesion:

1. Pour your primer into a clean paint tray lined with a disposable liner.

2. Using a high-quality angled paintbrush, cut in around the edges of the wall, applying a thin, even coat of primer along the baseboards, trim, and any other areas that a roller cannot easily reach.

3. Once you've cut in, switch to a paint roller with a 3/8" to 1/2" nap cover, and begin applying the primer to the main surface of the wall.

4. Work in small, manageable sections, using long, even strokes to apply a thin, uniform coat of primer across the entire surface.

5. Overlap each pass slightly to ensure consistent coverage and minimize the appearance of roller marks or edges.

6. Allow the primer to dry completely according to the manufacturer's instructions before applying paint.

Step 4: Painting the Wall

With the primer applied and fully dried, you're ready to paint your repaired plaster wall:

1. Pour your chosen interior paint into a clean paint tray lined with a new disposable liner.

2. Using a fresh angled paintbrush, cut in around the edges of the wall, just as you did with the primer.

3. Switch to a clean paint roller with a 3/8" to 1/2" nap cover, and begin applying the paint to the main surface of the wall, working in small, manageable sections.

4. Use long, even strokes to apply a thin, uniform coat of paint, overlapping each pass slightly to ensure consistent coverage.

5. Depending on the paint's opacity and the color of the primer, you may need to apply a second coat for full, even coverage. Allow the first coat to dry completely before applying the second coat, following the same technique as the first.

Step 5: Cleaning Up and Removing Tape
After the final coat of paint has dried completely, it's time to clean up your work area and remove any painter's tape:

1. Carefully remove the painter's tape from the baseboards, trim, and other adjacent surfaces, pulling it away from the wall at a 45-degree angle to avoid peeling off any fresh paint.

2. Dispose of any used drop cloths, plastic sheeting, or paint tray liners.

3. Clean your paintbrushes, roller covers, and other tools with warm, soapy water (for latex-based paints) or the appropriate solvent (for oil-based paints).

4. Allow the painted surface to cure fully according to the manufacturer's instructions before hanging any decor or returning furniture to the room.

By following these steps and using high-quality materials, you'll achieve a smooth, professional-looking finish on your repaired plaster walls that will stand the test of time. Priming and painting not only enhance the aesthetic appeal of your space but also help to protect your plaster walls from future damage or wear. With your newly refreshed walls, you can sit back, relax, and enjoy the fruits of your labor, knowing that you've accomplished a significant home improvement project with skill and precision.

Blending the Repaired Area with the Surrounding Wall

After priming and painting your repaired plaster wall, you may notice that the newly repaired area stands out from the surrounding wall, even if you've used the same paint color. This is because the texture and sheen of the repaired area can differ slightly from the original wall surface. To create a seamless, cohesive appearance, it's essential to blend the repaired area with the surrounding wall. In this section, we'll discuss various techniques for achieving a smooth, uniform transition between the repaired plaster and the original wall surface.

Technique 1: Feathering the Edges
One of the most effective ways to blend a repaired area with the surrounding wall is to feather the edges of the repair during the skim coating process:

1. When applying the final coat of skim coating compound, use a wider taping knife or trowel (12" to 14") to feather the edges of the repair, gradually tapering the thickness of the compound as you approach the surrounding wall.

2. Use long, smooth strokes to blend the edges of the repair seamlessly with the original surface, creating a gradual transition that's difficult to detect.

3. Sand the feathered edges with a fine-grit sandpaper (220-grit or higher) to further smooth and blend the transition.

Technique 2: Texturing the Repaired Area

If the surrounding wall has a distinct texture, such as a knockdown or orange peel finish, you may need to texture the repaired area to match:

1. After the final coat of skim coating compound has dried and been sanded, apply a thin layer of drywall texture spray or compound to the repaired area, using a texture sprayer, roller, or brush, depending on the desired effect.

2. Use a drywall knife, trowel, or specialty texture tool to create a texture that closely matches the surrounding wall.

3. Allow the texture to dry completely, then prime and paint the area as described in the previous section.

Technique 3: Blending Paint

In some cases, you may be able to blend the repaired area with the surrounding wall by carefully manipulating the paint:

1. After priming the repaired area, apply a coat of paint to the entire wall, including the repaired section.

2. While the paint is still wet, use a dry brush technique to feather the edges of the repaired area, gently brushing from the wet paint over the edge of the repair and onto the surrounding wall.

3. This technique can help to soften the transition between the repaired area and the original surface, creating a more seamless blend.

4. If necessary, apply a second coat of paint, using the same dry brush technique to further blend the edges.

Technique 4: Using Glaze or Faux Finishing Techniques
For more challenging situations, or to add a decorative element to your walls, you may consider using glaze or faux finishing techniques to blend the repaired area:

1. After priming and painting the entire wall, apply a tinted glaze or translucent faux finishing compound to the repaired area, using a specialty brush, sponge, or rag to create a mottled or textured effect that mimics the surrounding wall.

2. Blend the edges of the glazed area with the surrounding wall, using a clean, dry brush or rag to soften the transition.

3. Allow the glaze or faux finish to dry completely before applying a clear sealer, if desired, to protect the finish.

Tips for Successful Blending:
1. Always work in good lighting conditions to ensure that you can accurately assess the blending process and make any necessary adjustments.

2. Take your time and work patiently, as blending often requires a delicate touch and multiple layers to achieve a seamless result.

3. Practice your chosen blending technique on a scrap piece of drywall or poster board before attempting it on your repaired wall to build confidence and refine your skills.

4. If you're not satisfied with the initial blending results, allow the area to dry completely before attempting to re-blend or touch up the transition.

By using one or more of these blending techniques, you can create a smooth, seamless transition between your repaired plaster area and the surrounding wall. A well-blended repair will be virtually undetectable, ensuring that your walls look flawless and professionally finished. With patience, practice, and attention to detail, you can achieve outstanding results that will showcase your skill and elevate the overall appearance of your space.

Cleaning Up and Maintaining Your Tools

After completing your plaster wall repair and painting project, it's crucial to properly clean and maintain your tools to ensure their longevity and performance. Neglecting to clean your tools can lead to the buildup of dried compound, paint, or other materials, which can affect the quality of your work and shorten the lifespan of your equipment. In this section, we'll provide a detailed guide on how to clean and maintain your plaster repair and painting tools, so they remain in top condition for future projects.

Cleaning Plaster Repair Tools:
1. Taping Knives and Trowels:
- Scrape off any excess joint compound or plaster using a putty knife or a flat edge.
- Rinse the tools under running water, using a stiff-bristled brush to remove any remaining residue.
- For stubborn buildup, soak the tools in warm, soapy water for 10-15 minutes before scrubbing.
- Dry the tools thoroughly with a clean cloth to prevent rust or corrosion.

2. Hawks and Mud Pans:
- Remove any excess joint compound or plaster using a putty knife or trowel.
- Rinse the hawk or mud pan under running water, using a stiff-bristled brush to scrub away any remaining material.
- For tougher residue, fill the hawk or mud pan with warm, soapy water and allow it to soak for 10-15 minutes before scrubbing.

- Dry the tools completely with a clean cloth to prevent rust or warping.

3. Sandpaper and Sanding Tools:
- Brush off any loose dust or debris from the sandpaper or sanding tool using a dry, stiff-bristled brush.
- For reusable sanding sponges or pads, rinse them under running water, squeezing gently to remove any embedded dust or compound.
- Allow the sanding tools to air dry completely before storing them.

Cleaning Painting Tools:

1. Paintbrushes:
- Remove as much excess paint as possible by brushing the paintbrush against a piece of newspaper or cardboard.
- Rinse the brush under running water, using your fingers to gently work out any remaining paint from the bristles.
- For latex paint, use warm, soapy water to clean the brush; for oil-based paint, use the appropriate solvent (e.g., mineral spirits) as directed by the manufacturer.
- Reshape the bristles and allow the brush to air dry completely before storing it.

2. Paint Rollers:
- Remove excess paint from the roller by rolling it against a piece of newspaper or cardboard until no more paint comes off.
- Rinse the roller under running water, squeezing gently to remove any embedded paint.

- For latex paint, use warm, soapy water to clean the roller; for oil-based paint, use the appropriate solvent as directed by the manufacturer.
- Allow the roller to air dry completely before storing it.

3. Paint Trays and Liners:
- Pour any unused paint back into its original container for storage.
- Scrape off any excess paint from the tray or liner using a putty knife or trowel.
- Rinse the tray or liner under running water, using a stiff-bristled brush to remove any remaining paint.
- For latex paint, use warm, soapy water to clean the tray or liner; for oil-based paint, use the appropriate solvent as directed by the manufacturer.
- Allow the tray or liner to air dry completely before storing it.

Maintaining Your Tools:

1. Storage:
- Store your tools in a clean, dry place, away from direct sunlight or extreme temperatures.
- Hang brushes and rollers vertically to maintain their shape and prevent damage to the bristles or nap.
- Keep taping knives, trowels, and hawks organized in a toolbox or on a pegboard to prevent damage or loss.

2. Inspection:
- Before each use, inspect your tools for any signs of wear, damage, or rust.

- Replace any tools that are excessively worn, bent, or corroded to ensure the best possible results.

3. Lubrication:
- For tools with moving parts, such as scissors or utility knives, apply a small amount of lubricant (e.g., WD-40) to the pivot points to ensure smooth operation and prevent rust.

4. Sharpening:
- Regularly sharpen the blades of your utility knives, scissors, or any other cutting tools to maintain their effectiveness and precision.
- Use a sharpening stone or a professional sharpening service to keep your blades in top condition.

By following these cleaning and maintenance guidelines, you'll extend the life of your plaster repair and painting tools, ensuring that they remain in excellent condition for future projects. Well-maintained tools not only perform better but also contribute to a more professional-looking finish, as they apply materials more evenly and consistently. Investing a little time and effort into caring for your tools will pay off in the long run, saving you money on replacements and ensuring that you always have reliable, high-quality equipment on hand for your home improvement needs.

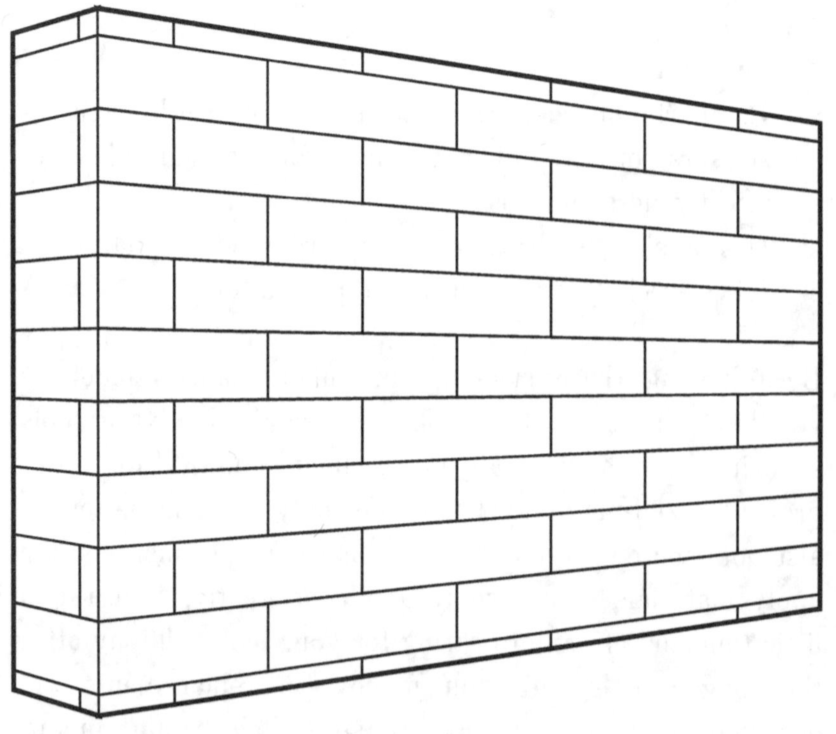

Chapter 6
Troubleshooting Common Issues
Dealing with Uneven or Sagging Plaster

Uneven or sagging plaster is a common issue faced by many homeowners, particularly in older homes with aging plaster walls. These issues can be caused by a variety of factors, such as moisture damage, structural settling, or poor installation techniques. Addressing uneven or sagging plaster can be challenging, but with the right approach and techniques, you can successfully repair these issues and restore your walls to their former glory. In this section, we'll provide a detailed guide on how to identify, assess, and repair uneven or sagging plaster walls.

Identifying Uneven or Sagging Plaster:

1. Visual Inspection:
- Examine your plaster walls carefully, looking for any areas that appear to be bulging, sagging, or uneven.
- Pay particular attention to areas around windows, doors, and corners, as these are common locations for plaster issues.
- Look for cracks, gaps, or separations between the plaster and the underlying lath or framing.

2. Tactile Inspection:
- Gently press on the surface of the plaster in various locations, feeling for any soft, spongy, or unstable areas.
- If the plaster feels loose or shifts under pressure, it may indicate that the plaster has separated from the lath or framing.

3. Level Check:

- Use a long, straight edge (such as a level or a straightedge) to check the evenness of your plaster walls.
- Place the straight edge vertically or horizontally against the wall, looking for any gaps or unevenness along its length.
- If the plaster is significantly uneven or sagging, it will be apparent when compared against the straight edge.

Assessing the Severity of the Issue:

1. Minor Unevenness:

- If the unevenness or sagging is minimal (less than 1/4 inch), it may be possible to repair the issue with skim coating techniques, as described in earlier chapters.
- Minor unevenness can often be corrected by applying multiple thin coats of joint compound, sanding between each coat, and blending the repaired area with the surrounding wall.

2. Moderate Unevenness:

- If the unevenness or sagging is more significant (between 1/4 inch and 1/2 inch), a more extensive repair may be necessary.
- Moderate unevenness may require the use of plaster washers or furring strips to provide additional support and even out the surface before skim coating.

3. Severe Unevenness or Sagging:

- If the unevenness or sagging is severe (greater than 1/2 inch), or if the plaster has completely separated from the lath or framing, a full plaster replacement may be necessary.
- In these cases, it's often best to consult with a professional plasterer or contractor to assess the situation and determine the most appropriate course of action.

Repairing Uneven or Sagging Plaster:
1. Minor Unevenness:

- Follow the skim coating techniques described in earlier chapters to apply multiple thin coats of joint compound over the uneven area.
- Sand between each coat, gradually building up the surface until it is level and even with the surrounding wall.
- Prime and paint the repaired area, blending it with the surrounding wall as described in Chapter 6.

2. Moderate Unevenness:

- If the plaster is moderately uneven or sagging, you may need to use plaster washers or furring strips to provide additional support before skim coating.
- Plaster washers are metal discs with perforated centers that are used to secure loose plaster to the underlying lath or framing. To install plaster washers:

a. Drill pilot holes through the plaster and into the lath or framing at regular intervals across the affected area.

b. Insert plaster washers into the pilot holes, and secure them with screws.

c. Skim coat over the plaster washers, building up the surface until it is level and even with the surrounding wall.

- Furring strips are thin strips of wood or metal that are used to create a new, even surface over severely uneven or sagging plaster. To install furring strips:

a. Remove any loose or severely damaged plaster from the affected area.

b. Attach furring strips to the underlying framing, running them perpendicular to the direction of the framing and spacing them evenly across the area.

c. Attach metal lath or plaster backer board to the furring strips, creating a new, stable surface for the plaster repair.

d. Apply a base coat of plaster over the metal lath or backer board, followed by finish coats and skim coating as needed to achieve a smooth, even surface.

3. Severe Unevenness or Sagging:

- In cases of severe unevenness or sagging, where the plaster has completely separated from the lath or framing, a full plaster replacement may be necessary.
- This process involves removing the damaged plaster, repairing or replacing any damaged lath or framing, and installing new plaster from scratch.
- Due to the complexity and skill required for a full plaster replacement, it is often best to hire a professional plasterer or contractor to handle this type of repair.

Preventing Future Issues:

1. Address Moisture Problems:

- Identify and repair any sources of moisture damage, such as leaks, high humidity, or poor ventilation, to prevent further plaster deterioration.

2. Monitor Structural Issues:

- Keep an eye out for any signs of structural settling or movement, such as new cracks or unevenness in your plaster walls.
- If you suspect a structural issue, consult with a professional contractor or structural engineer to assess the situation and recommend any necessary repairs.

3. Maintain Your Plaster Walls:

- Regularly inspect your plaster walls for any signs of damage, unevenness, or sagging.
- Address any issues promptly to prevent them from worsening over time.
- Consider applying a protective coating, such as a plaster sealer or paint, to help protect your plaster walls from moisture, wear, and tear.

By understanding how to identify, assess, and repair uneven or sagging plaster, you'll be better equipped to tackle these common issues and maintain the beauty and integrity of your plaster walls. Whether you choose to repair the issues yourself or hire a professional, addressing uneven or sagging plaster promptly and effectively will help to ensure the longevity and performance of your walls for years to come.

Fixing Bubbling or Peeling Skim Coating

Bubbling or peeling skim coating is a frustrating issue that can occur after applying a fresh layer of joint compound or plaster to your walls. This problem can be caused by various factors, such as improper surface preparation, application techniques, or environmental conditions. In this section, we'll dive into the causes of bubbling or peeling skim coating and provide a step-by-step guide on how to fix these issues to achieve a smooth, durable finish.

Understanding the Causes:

1. Poor Surface Preparation:

- Applying skim coating over a dirty, greasy, or glossy surface can prevent proper adhesion, leading to bubbling or peeling.
- Failing to prime the surface adequately before skim coating can also result in poor bonding and subsequent issues.

2. Incorrect Mixing:

- Mixing the joint compound or plaster inconsistently or with the wrong ratio of water can lead to a weak, unstable mixture that is prone to bubbling or peeling.
- Over-mixing the compound can introduce excess air bubbles, which may expand and cause bubbling as the skim coat dries.

3. Thick Application:

- Applying the skim coating too thickly can lead to uneven drying and shrinkage, which may cause bubbling or peeling as the surface cures.

- Thick coats also take longer to dry, increasing the risk of moisture-related issues.

4. High Humidity or Moisture:
- Applying skim coating in high humidity environments or areas prone to moisture can slow down the drying process and lead to bubbling or peeling.
- If the underlying surface is damp or contains excess moisture, it can cause the skim coating to fail.

5. Inadequate Drying Time:
- Not allowing sufficient drying time between coats can trap moisture beneath the surface, causing bubbling or peeling as the skim coating cures.
- Applying paint or other finishes before the skim coating has fully dried can also lead to adhesion issues.

Fixing Bubbling or Peeling Skim Coating:
1. Assess the Extent of the Problem:
- Examine the affected area closely to determine the severity and scope of the bubbling or peeling.
- If the issue is localized and minor, spot repairs may be sufficient. However, if the problem is widespread or severe, a more extensive repair may be necessary.

2. Remove Loose or Damaged Material:
- Using a putty knife or scraper, carefully remove any loose, bubbling, or peeling skim coating.
- Be cautious not to damage the underlying surface or remove any well-adhered skim coating.

- If the bubbling or peeling extends through multiple coats, you may need to remove all affected layers down to a stable, well-bonded surface.

3. Clean and Prepare the Surface:
- Thoroughly clean the exposed surface, removing any dust, debris, or residue from the removal process.
- If the underlying surface is greasy or glossy, use a degreaser or sand the area lightly to promote better adhesion.
- If the surface is porous or heavily damaged, consider applying a primer or sealer to create a stable base for the new skim coating.

4. Mix the Skim Coating Compound Properly:
- Follow the manufacturer's instructions carefully when mixing the joint compound or plaster.
- Ensure that the mixture is smooth, lump-free, and at the proper consistency for application.
- Avoid over-mixing, as this can introduce excess air bubbles and weaken the mixture.

5. Apply the Skim Coating in Thin, Even Layers:
- Using a clean putty knife or trowel, apply the skim coating in thin, even layers over the prepared surface.
- Focus on building up the surface gradually, rather than attempting to fill the entire area in one thick coat.
- Feather the edges of the repaired area to blend seamlessly with the surrounding surface.

6. Allow Adequate Drying Time:

- Follow the manufacturer's recommendations for drying times between coats and before sanding or painting.
- Ensure that each coat is fully dry before applying the next layer, and allow the final coat to cure completely before proceeding with any additional steps.
- If possible, control the humidity and temperature in the room to promote optimal drying conditions.

7. Sand and Smooth the Repaired Area:

- Once the final coat of skim coating is completely dry, sand the repaired area with a fine-grit sandpaper (120-150 grit) to achieve a smooth, even finish.
- Be careful not to over-sand, as this can expose the underlying layers or create uneven spots.
- Wipe away any dust or debris with a clean, damp cloth after sanding.

8. Prime and Paint:

- Apply a quality primer over the repaired area to seal the surface and promote even paint adhesion.
- Once the primer is dry, paint the area to match the surrounding wall, using the techniques described in Chapter 6 to blend the repair seamlessly.

Preventing Future Issues:

1. Ensure Proper Surface Preparation:

- Always clean and prime surfaces thoroughly before applying skim coating to promote optimal adhesion and prevent bubbling or peeling.

2. Use High-Quality Materials:

- Choose high-quality joint compounds, plasters, and primers specifically designed for your application to minimize the risk of compatibility issues or product failures.

3. Follow Manufacturer's Instructions:

- Carefully read and follow the manufacturer's guidelines for mixing, application, and drying times to ensure the best possible results.

4. Control Environmental Factors:

- When possible, maintain a stable, moderate humidity level and temperature during the application and drying process to promote proper curing and minimize the risk of moisture-related issues.

By understanding the causes of bubbling or peeling skim coating and following these step-by-step instructions for fixing and preventing these issues, you can achieve a smooth, durable finish that will last for years to come. Remember to work patiently, pay attention to detail, and always prioritize proper surface preparation and application techniques to ensure the best possible results.

Addressing Cracks That Reappear After Repair

Few things are more frustrating than taking the time to carefully repair a crack in your plaster wall, only to have it reappear days or weeks later. Recurring cracks can be caused by a variety of factors, ranging from structural issues to improper repair techniques. In this section, we'll explore the common causes of recurring cracks and provide a detailed guide on how to address these issues effectively to achieve a long-lasting, stable repair.

Understanding the Causes:

1. Structural Movement:

- Cracks that reappear after repair may be a sign of ongoing structural movement or settling in your home.
- This movement can be caused by factors such as foundation shifts, soil settlement, or changes in moisture content around your home's structure.
- If the underlying structural issue is not addressed, cracks may continue to form even after repeated repairs.

2. Improper Repair Techniques:

- Using the wrong type of repair material, such as a non-flexible filler or a compound that is too thick, can lead to recurring cracks.
- Failing to properly prepare the surface or apply the repair material correctly can also result in a weak, unstable repair that is prone to cracking.
- Skipping crucial steps, such as priming or allowing adequate drying time, can compromise the integrity of the repair and lead to recurring issues.

3. Insufficient Reinforcement:
- If the crack is wide, deep, or located in an area subject to stress or movement, a simple fill and cover repair may not be enough to prevent it from reappearing.
- Failing to use reinforcing materials, such as mesh tape or fiberglass tape, can leave the repair vulnerable to cracking under pressure.

4. Environmental Factors:
- Fluctuations in temperature and humidity can cause plaster to expand and contract, leading to recurring cracks.
- If your home is prone to extreme temperature changes or high humidity levels, it may be more susceptible to recurring plaster cracks.

5. Poor Original Installation:
- In some cases, recurring cracks may be a result of poor original plaster installation or underlying structural issues that have been present since the building's construction.
- If the original plaster work was subpar or the structure was not properly designed to accommodate movement, cracks may reappear despite your best repair efforts.

Addressing Recurring Cracks:

1. Assess the Underlying Cause:
- Before attempting to repair a recurring crack, take the time to investigate and identify the underlying cause.
- Look for signs of structural movement, such as doors or windows that no longer fit properly, sloping floors, or cracks in the foundation.

- Consider the location and pattern of the cracks, as well as any recent changes or events that may have contributed to their formation.

2. Address Structural Issues:
- If you suspect that structural movement is the cause of your recurring cracks, it's essential to address these issues before attempting any further repairs.
- Consult with a professional contractor, structural engineer, or foundation specialist to assess the situation and recommend appropriate solutions.
- Depending on the nature and severity of the structural issue, you may need to undertake foundation repairs, install structural reinforcement, or make other modifications to stabilize your home.

3. Use Flexible Repair Materials:
- When repairing recurring cracks, choose flexible repair materials that can accommodate minor movements and prevent future cracking.
- Elastomeric fillers, such as acrylic latex caulk or elastomeric patching compounds, are designed to flex and stretch with the movement of the plaster, reducing the risk of cracks reappearing.
- Avoid using rigid, inflexible materials like spackling paste or drywall joint compound, as these are more likely to crack under stress.

4. Reinforce the Repair:
- For larger or more persistent cracks, consider reinforcing the repair to provide additional stability and prevent future cracking.

- Apply a layer of mesh tape or fiberglass tape over the crack before filling it with the repair material. This will help to distribute stress and prevent the crack from reopening.
- For deep or wide cracks, consider using a backing material, such as a foam backer rod or a strip of drywall tape, to fill the void before applying the repair material.

5. Follow Proper Repair Techniques:

- To ensure a long-lasting, stable repair, follow the proper techniques for preparing the surface, applying the repair material, and allowing adequate drying time.
- Clean the crack and surrounding area thoroughly, removing any loose debris or dust.
- Prime the surface before applying the repair material to promote better adhesion and prevent future cracking.
- Apply the repair material in thin, even layers, allowing each layer to dry completely before adding the next.
- Feather the edges of the repair to create a smooth, seamless transition with the surrounding plaster.

6. Control Environmental Factors:

- To minimize the impact of temperature and humidity fluctuations on your plaster walls, take steps to control these environmental factors.
- Use a dehumidifier to maintain a stable, moderate humidity level in your home, particularly in damp or moisture-prone areas.
- Ensure that your home is properly insulated and sealed to minimize drafts and temperature variations that can contribute to plaster movement and cracking.

- Consider installing a programmable thermostat to maintain a consistent temperature throughout the day and night.

7. Monitor and Maintain:
- After completing the repair, keep a close eye on the area to monitor for any signs of cracking or movement.
- If cracks do reappear, address them promptly using the same techniques and materials to prevent them from worsening over time.
- Regularly inspect your plaster walls for any new or developing issues, and address them proactively to maintain the integrity and beauty of your home.

Preventing Recurring Cracks:
1. Address Structural Issues Promptly:
- If you suspect that your home has underlying structural issues, address them promptly to prevent recurring plaster cracks and other potential damage.

2. Maintain Stable Environmental Conditions:
- Take steps to control humidity and temperature levels in your home to minimize the risk of plaster movement and cracking.

3. Use Appropriate Materials:
- When making repairs or installing new plaster, choose high-quality, flexible materials that are designed to accommodate minor movements and prevent cracking.

4. Hire Qualified Professionals:

- If you are unsure about the cause of your recurring cracks or lack the experience to make proper repairs, consider hiring a qualified professional plasterer or contractor to assess the situation and recommend appropriate solutions.

By understanding the causes of recurring plaster cracks and following these guidelines for addressing and preventing them, you can ensure that your repairs are long-lasting, stable, and effective. Remember to approach each situation with patience, attention to detail, and a commitment to finding the best possible solution for your unique circumstances. With the right knowledge, tools, and techniques, you can keep your plaster walls looking beautiful and crack-free for years to come.

Chapter 6
Advanced Techniques and Speciality Situations

Repairing Ornamental Plaster Features

Ornamental plaster features, such as cornices, medallions, and moldings, add character, elegance, and historical charm to many homes. However, these intricate elements can be particularly challenging to repair when damaged due to their complex designs, delicate surfaces, and the need to maintain their aesthetic integrity. In this section, we'll explore advanced techniques for repairing ornamental plaster features, ensuring that you can restore these beautiful elements to their original glory.

Assessing the Damage:

1. Type of Damage:
- Carefully examine the ornamental plaster feature to determine the type and extent of the damage.
- Common issues include cracks, chips, breaks, or missing sections.
- Identify any underlying causes of the damage, such as moisture intrusion, structural movement, or impact damage.

2. Structural Integrity:
- Assess the overall structural integrity of the ornamental feature.
- Check for any signs of sagging, separation from the wall or ceiling, or instability.

- If the feature appears to be structurally compromised, it may require more extensive repairs or even replacement.

3. Material Composition:
- Determine the material composition of the ornamental plaster feature.
- Traditional ornamental plaster is typically made from gypsum plaster, lime plaster, or a combination of both.
- Some newer ornamental features may be made from lighter-weight materials, such as polyurethane or resin.

Preparing for the Repair:

1. Documentation:
- Before beginning any repair work, thoroughly document the ornamental feature.
- Take detailed photographs from multiple angles to capture the design, dimensions, and any intricate details.
- Create sketches or measurements of the feature to help guide your repair work.

2. Clean the Surface:
- Gently clean the surface of the ornamental feature, removing any dirt, dust, or debris.
- Use a soft-bristled brush, compressed air, or a vacuum with a brush attachment to avoid damaging the delicate surface.
- If necessary, use a mild detergent solution to remove any stubborn grime, ensuring that the surface is thoroughly dried afterward.

3. Stabilize Loose or Fragile Areas:

- If any parts of the ornamental feature are loose, fragile, or in danger of falling, stabilize them before proceeding with the repair.
- Use a compatible adhesive, such as a polyvinyl acetate (PVA) glue or an epoxy resin, to secure loose pieces.
- If necessary, provide temporary support using props, braces, or clamps while the adhesive dries.

Repairing Cracks, Chips, and Small Breaks:

1. Clean the Damaged Area:

- Remove any loose plaster, paint, or debris from the damaged area using a small chisel, utility knife, or sandpaper.
- Ensure that the edges of the damaged area are clean and stable.

2. Mix the Repair Material:

- Select an appropriate repair material based on the composition of the original plaster and the extent of the damage.
- For small cracks and chips, a fine surface filler or patching compound may be sufficient.
- For larger breaks or missing sections, a plaster-based repair material, such as a casting plaster or a molding plaster, may be necessary.
- Mix the repair material according to the manufacturer's instructions, ensuring a smooth, lump-free consistency.

3. Apply the Repair Material:

- Using a small spatula, palette knife, or modeling tool, apply the repair material to the damaged area.
- For cracks and chips, fill the void completely, slightly overfilling to allow for shrinkage.
- For breaks or missing sections, build up the repair material gradually, using the photographs and sketches as a guide to recreate the original shape and details.
- Use a damp sponge or fine sandpaper to smooth and blend the repair with the surrounding surface.

4. Allow to Dry and Cure:

- Allow the repair material to dry and cure completely according to the manufacturer's instructions.
- Drying times may vary depending on the type of material used, the thickness of the repair, and the ambient humidity and temperature.

5. Sand and Refine:

- Once the repair material is fully cured, use fine sandpaper or a sanding sponge to gently sand the repaired area, smoothing any rough spots or imperfections.
- Take care not to sand too aggressively, as this may damage the surrounding plaster or alter the original profile of the ornamental feature.

6. Prime and Paint:

- Apply a compatible primer to the repaired area, ensuring thorough coverage and even application.

- Once the primer is dry, paint the repaired area to match the surrounding plaster, using thin, even coats to build up the color gradually.
- If necessary, use a small artist's brush or a detailing tool to recreate any intricate paint patterns or highlights.

Recreating Missing Sections:

1. Create a Template:
- If a significant portion of the ornamental feature is missing, create a template to guide the recreation process.
- Use the photographs and sketches to trace the outline of the missing section onto a piece of cardboard, plastic, or metal.
- Cut out the template, ensuring that it accurately represents the size, shape, and profile of the missing section.

2. Prepare a Mold:
- Using the template as a guide, create a mold of the missing section using a flexible molding material, such as silicone rubber or alginate.
- Press the molding material firmly against the template and the surrounding plaster, ensuring that all details and contours are captured.
- Allow the mold to set and cure according to the manufacturer's instructions.

3. Cast the Replacement Piece:
- Once the mold is fully cured, use a compatible casting material, such as plaster or resin, to cast the replacement piece.

- Mix the casting material according to the manufacturer's instructions, ensuring a smooth, pourable consistency.
- Pour the casting material into the mold, tapping gently to release any air bubbles.
- Allow the casting to set and harden completely before removing it from the mold.

4. Attach the Replacement Piece:
- Clean and prepare the edges of the original plaster and the replacement piece, ensuring a snug, secure fit.
- Apply a compatible adhesive to the back of the replacement piece and the corresponding area on the original plaster.
- Press the replacement piece firmly into place, using clamps or temporary supports if necessary to hold it securely while the adhesive dries.

5. Blend and Finish:
- Once the adhesive has dried completely, use a compatible filler or patching compound to blend the edges of the replacement piece with the surrounding plaster.
- Sand, prime, and paint the repaired area as described in the previous section, taking care to match the color, sheen, and texture of the original plaster.

Preventing Future Damage:
1. Address Underlying Issues:
- If the damage to the ornamental plaster feature was caused by an underlying issue, such as moisture intrusion or structural movement, address these problems promptly to prevent future damage.

2. Regular Maintenance:

- Protect ornamental plaster features from damage by performing regular maintenance, such as dusting, cleaning, and touching up paint as needed.
- Avoid hanging heavy objects or applying excessive force to the plaster features, as this can cause cracking, chipping, or breakage.

3. Professional Assistance:

- If you are unsure about the repair process or encounter a particularly challenging situation, consider seeking the assistance of a professional plaster artisan or restoration specialist.
- These experts have the knowledge, skills, and experience to assess the damage, recommend appropriate repair techniques, and ensure that the ornamental feature is restored to its original beauty.

By following these advanced techniques and taking a thoughtful, methodical approach to repairing ornamental plaster features, you can successfully restore these beautiful architectural elements, preserving their historical value and enhancing the character of your home. Remember to work patiently, pay close attention to detail, and always prioritize the integrity and aesthetic of the original design. With the right tools, materials, and techniques, you can ensure that your ornamental plaster features continue to captivate and inspire for generations to come.

Working with Historic Plaster Walls

Historic plaster walls are a testament to the craftsmanship and materials of the past, offering a unique glimpse into the architectural heritage of our built environment. Preserving and repairing these walls requires a specialized approach that prioritizes the retention of original materials, techniques, and aesthetics. In this section, we'll delve into the intricacies of working with historic plaster walls, providing guidance on how to assess, repair, and maintain these irreplaceable features.

Understanding Historic Plaster:

1. Composition:

- Historic plaster walls are typically composed of three layers: the scratch coat, the brown coat, and the finish coat.
- The scratch coat is the first layer applied to the lath, providing a rough, keyed surface for the subsequent layers to adhere to.
- The brown coat is the second layer, which is used to establish the general shape and contours of the wall.
- The finish coat is the final, smooth layer that provides the decorative surface of the plaster wall.

2. Materials:

- Traditional historic plaster is made from a combination of lime, sand, water, and various additives, such as animal hair or straw, which help to reinforce the plaster and prevent cracking.

- Lime plaster is known for its durability, breathability, and self-healing properties, which contribute to its longevity and resilience.

3. Lath:

- Historic plaster walls are often supported by wooden lath, which is a series of thin, narrow strips of wood nailed horizontally across the wall studs.
- The spaces between the lath allow the wet plaster to key into the wood, creating a strong, mechanical bond between the plaster and the lath.

Assessing Historic Plaster Walls:
1. Condition Survey:

- Before undertaking any repair or restoration work, conduct a thorough condition survey of the historic plaster walls.
- Identify and document any areas of damage, deterioration, or alteration, such as cracks, bulges, separations, or missing sections.
- Note any sources of moisture, structural movement, or other factors that may be contributing to the deterioration of the plaster.

2. Material Analysis:

- Where possible, collect small samples of the historic plaster for material analysis.
- Laboratory testing can help to determine the composition of the plaster, including the proportions of lime, sand, and any additives used.

- This information is crucial for developing compatible repair materials and techniques that will not harm the original plaster.

3. Structural Assessment:
- Assess the overall structural stability of the historic plaster walls, paying particular attention to any areas of sagging, separation, or loss of adhesion to the lath.
- If necessary, consult with a structural engineer or historic preservation specialist to determine the best course of action for stabilizing and supporting the plaster walls.

Repairing Historic Plaster Walls:
1. Cleaning:
- Before beginning any repair work, gently clean the surface of the historic plaster walls to remove any dirt, dust, or debris.
- Use a soft-bristled brush, vacuum with a brush attachment, or compressed air to avoid damaging the delicate plaster surface.
- If necessary, use a mild, pH-neutral cleaner to remove any stubborn grime, ensuring that the surface is thoroughly rinsed and dried afterward.

2. Stabilization:
- If any areas of the historic plaster are loose, detached, or in danger of falling, stabilize them before proceeding with repairs.
- Use a compatible adhesive, such as a lime-based grout or injection mortar, to reattach loose plaster to the lath or underlying substrate.

- If necessary, provide temporary support using props, braces, or plaster washers while the adhesive sets.

3. Crack Repair:
- For hairline cracks or minor fissures, use a lime-based filler or patching compound to fill the voids, taking care to maintain the original surface texture and profile.
- For larger cracks or gaps, use a lime-based mortar or plaster mix to fill the voids in layers, allowing each layer to dry and shrink before applying the next.
- Once the repair material has dried completely, use a damp sponge or fine sandpaper to blend the repair with the surrounding plaster.

4. Replacing Missing Sections:
- If significant sections of the historic plaster are missing or beyond repair, replace them using traditional materials and techniques.
- Create a template of the missing section using photographs, sketches, or existing ornamental features as a guide.
- Mix a lime-based plaster that closely matches the composition and proportions of the original plaster, as determined through material analysis.
- Apply the plaster in layers, using the template to recreate the original contours and details of the missing section.
- Allow each layer to dry and cure before applying the next, finishing with a smooth, matched surface that blends seamlessly with the surrounding plaster.

5. Finishing:

- Once all repairs have been completed and the plaster has cured, apply a compatible lime-based finish coat to protect the surface and restore the original appearance of the wall.
- If necessary, match the color, texture, and sheen of the original plaster using natural pigments, aggregates, or other traditional techniques.
- Avoid using modern paints, sealers, or coatings that may trap moisture or compromise the breathability of the historic plaster.

Maintaining Historic Plaster Walls:

1. Environmental Control:

- Maintain a stable, moderate environment within the building to minimize the risk of moisture damage, thermal stress, or other factors that can contribute to plaster deterioration.
- Use a dehumidifier to control excess humidity, and ensure that the building is properly ventilated to prevent condensation and mold growth.

2. Regular Inspection:

- Conduct regular inspections of the historic plaster walls to identify any new or developing issues, such as cracks, staining, or loss of adhesion.
- Address any problems promptly using appropriate repair techniques to prevent further damage and maintain the integrity of the plaster.

3. Cleaning and Maintenance:

- Periodically clean the surface of the historic plaster walls using gentle, non-abrasive methods, such as dusting with a soft-bristled brush or vacuuming with a brush attachment.
- Avoid using harsh chemicals, abrasive cleaners, or excessive moisture, which can damage the delicate surface of the plaster.

4. Professional Consultation:

- When working with historic plaster walls, it is always advisable to consult with a professional conservator, restoration specialist, or historic preservation expert.
- These professionals can provide valuable guidance on assessment, repair techniques, material selection, and long-term maintenance strategies that are specific to your unique situation.

By understanding the composition, construction, and vulnerabilities of historic plaster walls, and by following these guidelines for assessment, repair, and maintenance, you can successfully preserve these irreplaceable features for future generations. Remember to approach each project with patience, care, and a deep respect for the craftsmanship and materials of the past. By prioritizing the retention of original fabric and using compatible techniques and materials, you can ensure that these architectural treasures continue to enrich our built heritage for years to come.

Integrating Plaster Repair with Other Wall Coverings

In many homes, plaster walls coexist with other wall coverings, such as wallpaper, paint, or decorative finishes. When repairing plaster in these situations, it's essential to consider how the repair process will integrate with the surrounding wall coverings, ensuring a seamless, cohesive appearance. In this section, we'll explore techniques for integrating plaster repair with various wall coverings, providing guidance on how to achieve a successful, long-lasting result.

Assessing the Wall Coverings:

1. Type of Wall Covering:
- Identify the type of wall covering surrounding the damaged plaster area, such as wallpaper, paint, or decorative finishes like Venetian plaster or textured coatings.
- Determine the age, condition, and adherence of the wall covering to the underlying plaster.
- Assess whether the wall covering will need to be removed, replaced, or repaired in conjunction with the plaster repair process.

2. Compatibility:
- Consider the compatibility of the plaster repair materials and techniques with the existing wall covering.
- Some wall coverings, such as certain types of wallpaper or delicate decorative finishes, may be sensitive to moisture, solvents, or abrasion, which could be involved in the plaster repair process.

- Select repair materials and methods that will not damage or compromise the integrity of the surrounding wall covering.

3. Aesthetic Considerations:
- Evaluate the visual impact of the plaster repair on the overall appearance of the wall covering.
- Consider factors such as color, texture, sheen, and pattern, and determine how the repaired area will blend with the existing wall covering.
- If necessary, plan to replicate or recreate any decorative elements or finishes that may be affected by the plaster repair process.

Repairing Plaster with Wallpaper:
1. Removing Wallpaper:
- If the wallpaper surrounding the damaged plaster area is in good condition and well-adhered, it may be possible to repair the plaster without removing the wallpaper.
- However, if the wallpaper is damaged, loose, or preventing access to the plaster substrate, it may be necessary to remove it before proceeding with the repair.
- Use a wallpaper steamer, scoring tool, or chemical stripper to carefully remove the wallpaper, taking care not to damage the underlying plaster.

2. Preparing the Surface:
- Once the damaged plaster area is exposed, prepare the surface for repair by removing any loose or crumbling material, cleaning the area, and priming the substrate if necessary.

- If the surrounding wallpaper has been removed, ensure that the edges of the repair area are smooth and level with the adjacent plaster surface.

3. Repairing the Plaster:
- Proceed with the plaster repair using appropriate materials and techniques, as described in earlier chapters.
- Take care to maintain the original surface profile and texture of the plaster, ensuring that the repair will blend seamlessly with the surrounding area.

4. Rehanging Wallpaper:
- If the wallpaper was removed for the repair process, rehang it once the plaster repair has been completed and the surface has been properly prepared.
- Ensure that the wallpaper adhesive is compatible with the repaired plaster surface, and take care to align patterns and match seams with the existing wallpaper.
- If necessary, touch up any areas where the wallpaper has been damaged or discolored during the repair process.

Repairing Plaster with Paint:
1. Removing Paint:
- If the paint surrounding the damaged plaster area is in good condition and well-adhered, it may be possible to repair the plaster without removing the paint.
- However, if the paint is cracked, flaking, or preventing access to the plaster substrate, it may be necessary to remove it before proceeding with the repair.

- Use a paint scraper, heat gun, or chemical stripper to carefully remove the paint, taking care not to damage the underlying plaster.

2. Preparing the Surface:

- Once the damaged plaster area is exposed, prepare the surface for repair by removing any loose or crumbling material, cleaning the area, and priming the substrate if necessary.
- If the surrounding paint has been removed, ensure that the edges of the repair area are smooth and level with the adjacent plaster surface.

3. Repairing the Plaster:

- Proceed with the plaster repair using appropriate materials and techniques, as described in earlier chapters.
- Take care to maintain the original surface profile and texture of the plaster, ensuring that the repair will blend seamlessly with the surrounding area.

4. Priming and Painting:

- Once the plaster repair has been completed and the surface has been properly prepared, prime the repaired area with a compatible primer to ensure proper adhesion of the paint.
- Apply the paint in thin, even coats, feathering the edges of the repair area to blend with the surrounding paint.
- If necessary, apply additional coats of paint to achieve a uniform color and sheen, matching the repaired area to the existing wall surface.

Repairing Plaster with Decorative Finishes:
1. Identifying the Finish:
- If the damaged plaster area is surrounded by a decorative finish, such as Venetian plaster, textured coating, or faux finish, identify the specific type of finish and the materials and techniques used to create it.
- Consult with a professional decorative finish artist or conservator, if necessary, to determine the best approach for integrating the plaster repair with the existing finish.

2. Preparing the Surface:
- Carefully remove any loose or damaged decorative finish material surrounding the plaster repair area, taking care not to damage the underlying plaster substrate.
- Prepare the surface for repair by cleaning the area and priming the substrate if necessary.

3. Repairing the Plaster:
- Proceed with the plaster repair using appropriate materials and techniques, as described in earlier chapters.
- Take care to maintain the original surface profile and texture of the plaster, ensuring that the repair will provide a suitable base for the reapplication of the decorative finish.

4. Recreating the Decorative Finish:
- Once the plaster repair has been completed and the surface has been properly prepared, recreate the decorative finish over the repaired area using materials and techniques that match the existing finish.

- Work carefully to blend the edges of the repaired area
  with the surrounding finish, replicating any patterns,
  textures, or color variations to achieve a seamless
  integration.
- If necessary, consult with a professional decorative finish
  artist to ensure that the repaired area is
  indistinguishable from the original finish.

By considering the unique challenges and opportunities
presented by different wall coverings, and by following these
guidelines for integrating plaster repair with wallpaper,
paint, and decorative finishes, you can successfully restore
damaged plaster surfaces while maintaining the overall
aesthetic and integrity of your interior spaces. Remember to
approach each project with care, patience, and a commitment
to achieving the best possible results, seeking professional
guidance and expertise when necessary to ensure a flawless,
long-lasting repair.

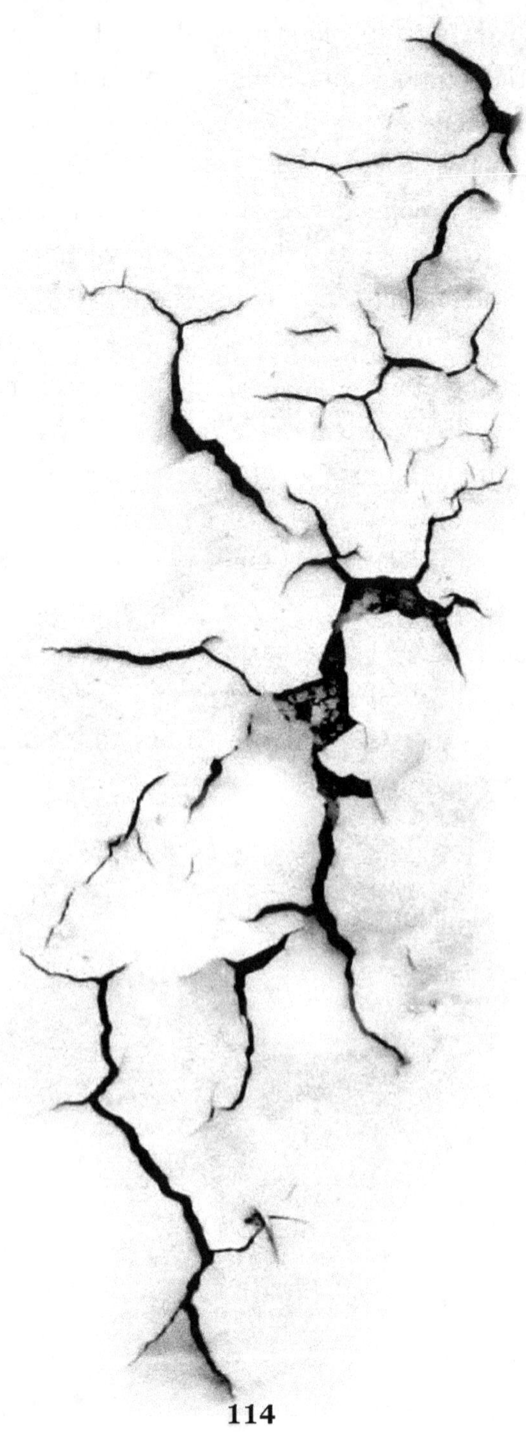

Conclusion

Throughout this comprehensive guide, we've explored the world of plaster wall repair and skim coating, providing you with the knowledge, skills, and techniques necessary to tackle a wide range of challenges and achieve professional-quality results.

We began by emphasizing the importance of understanding the unique characteristics and vulnerabilities of plaster walls, and the value of preserving these timeless architectural features. From there, we delved into the essential tools and materials required for successful plaster repair and skim coating, offering guidance on how to select the best products for your specific needs and budget.

As we progressed through the chapters, we provided detailed, step-by-step instructions for repairing cracks, holes, and other common plaster wall issues, as well as advanced techniques for addressing more complex problems like uneven surfaces, water damage, and structural instability. We also explored the art of skim coating, teaching you how to achieve a flawless, glass-smooth finish that will transform the look and feel of your interior spaces.

Along the way, we shared invaluable tips, tricks, and insider secrets for streamlining your workflow, avoiding common pitfalls, and achieving the best possible outcomes. From proper surface preparation and material mixing to creative problem-solving and finishing touches, we covered every aspect of the plaster repair and skim coating process, empowering you to tackle projects with confidence and finesse.

Celebrating Your Accomplishment and Enjoying Your Smooth, Repaired Plaster Walls

As you close the pages of this book and survey the smooth, flawless plaster walls that stand as a testament to your hard work and dedication, take a moment to celebrate your accomplishment. You've not only mastered the art of plaster repair and skim coating but also played a vital role in preserving the beauty, character, and integrity of your home.

The skills and knowledge you've acquired throughout this journey will serve you well for years to come, enabling you to maintain and enhance your plaster walls with ease and confidence. You'll be able to tackle future repair projects with poise and precision, and even share your expertise with friends, family, and neighbors who may seek your guidance and advice.

But perhaps most importantly, you'll be able to enjoy the fruits of your labor every day, as you bask in the warmth, elegance, and timeless charm of your beautifully restored plaster walls. Whether you're relaxing in your living room, entertaining guests in your dining area, or simply admiring the play of light across a perfectly smooth surface, you'll feel a deep sense of pride and satisfaction knowing that you've played a direct role in creating this stunning, inviting space.

So go ahead and revel in your achievement, and savor the joy and contentment that comes with a job well done. You've earned it through your patience, perseverance, and unwavering commitment to excellence. And as you move forward on your home improvement journey, remember that the skills and confidence you've gained through mastering plaster repair and skim coating will serve as a strong foundation for tackling even more ambitious projects in the future.

Congratulations on your success, and thank you for joining us on this rewarding and enriching journey. May your newly repaired and skim coated plaster walls stand as a lasting symbol of your accomplishment, and may they bring you joy, comfort, and inspiration for many years to come.

www.ingramcontent.com/pod-product-compliance
Lightning Source LLC
Chambersburg PA
CBHW071041250726

48653CB00005B/1940